The Babe, B.A.

by

Edward F. Benson

The Babe, B.A.
by Edward F. Benson

Copyright © 2023

All Rights reserved.

No part of this publication may be reproduced,
stored in a retrieval system, or transmitted in any
form or by any means, electronic, mechanical,
photocopying or Otherwise, without the written
permission of the publisher.
The author/editor asserts the moral right to
be identified as the author/editor of this work.

ISBN: 978-93-59958-75-0

Published by

DOUBLE 9 BOOKS

2/13-B, Ansari Road
Daryaganj, New Delhi – 110002
info@double9books.com
www.double9books.com
Tel. 011-40042856

This book is under public domain

ABOUT THE AUTHOR

Edward Frederic Benson OBE (24 July 1867 – 29 February 1940) was a novelist, biographer, memoirist, historian, and short story writer from the United Kingdom. E. F. Benson was the fifth child of Wellington College's headmaster, Edward White Benson (after chancellor of Lincoln Cathedral, Bishop of Truro, and Archbishop of Canterbury), and his wife, Mary Sidgwick ("Minnie"). E. F. Benson was the younger brother of Arthur Christopher Benson, who penned "Land of Hope and Glory," Robert Hugh Benson, who wrote several novels and Roman Catholic apologetic works, and Margaret Benson (Maggie), a novelist and amateur Egyptologist. Two other siblings perished when they were young. Benson had six children but no grandchildren. Benson attended Temple Grove School and subsequently Marlborough College, where he composed some of his early writings and based his novel David Blaize. He pursued his schooling at Cambridge's King's College. He was a member of the Pitt Club at Cambridge and later became an honorary fellow of Magdalene College. Benson was a gifted and prolific writer. Sketches from Marlborough, his first book, was published while he was still a student. He began his novel-writing career with the (then) fashionable controversial Dodo (1893), which was an instant success, and went on to write a range of satire, romantic and supernatural melodrama, and fantasy.

CONTENTS

DEDICATION

Dear Toby:

It is fitting, and I hope you will not feel it otherwise, that your name should appear on the forefront of this little book, for you know best how much good humour went to the making of it, and how when it was read piecemeal, as it was written, to you, your native politeness, which I cannot admire too much, more than once prompted you to laugh. (Advt.) You will remember, too, when I first mentioned the idea of it to you, that with some solemnity we procured a large sheet of foolscap paper, and a blue pencil, and then and there set ourselves to put down all the remarkable and stirring events which happened to us in those four years we spent together at Cambridge; how we failed egregiously to recollect anything remarkable or stirring—pardon me, we remembered one stirring event, but decided not to treat the world to it—which had come within our personal experience, and thereupon cast, or as you said, "speired" about for any remarkable and stirring incident, which had happened, not, alas, to us, but to anybody else soever. Here again I may recall to you that we drew blank, and our sheet of paper was still virgin white, our blue pencil as sharp as ever, and the book no nearer conception than before.

Then it was that the uncomfortable conviction dawned on us, gradually illuminating our minds as some cloudy rain-slanted morning grows clear to half-wakened eyes, that in the majority of cases, remarkable and stirring events do not befall the undergraduate, and that if the book was to be made at all, it must be made of homely, and I hope wholesome, ingredients, a cricket ball, a canoe, a football, a tripos, a don, a croquet mallet, a few undergraduates, a Greek play, some work, and so forth. For it seemed to us that the superficial enquirer—and you, I vow, are even more superficially-minded than I—finds that these things are common to the experience of most men, but that when you begin to deal in spiritualities, heroes, century-making captains of eleven, chess blues, and higher aspirations, you desert the normal plane for the super-normal, where people like you and me have no business to intrude.

So that, now it is complete, you will find therein neither births, deaths, nor marriages, and though the <u>Babe</u> himself may have waxed a little out of proportion to our original scheme—he ought, for instance, never to have played Rugby for his University, as savouring too much of the hero—I have retained for him to the end that futility of mind, and girt him about with that flippant atmosphere, in which the *truly heroic chokes and stifles. About the other characters I have no such confessions to make; they have successfully steered clear of all distinctions, bodily or mental; I have even omitted to state <u>Ealing's</u> place in the tripos, and for this reason. He ought to have done better than the <u>Babe</u>, but the <u>Babe</u> got a second, and this leaves only one class where Ealing's name would reasonably appear, and I altogether refuse to let him take a first.*

Good-bye for the present: but you will be home for leave, will you not, in a month?

Believe me, my dear Toby,
Ever your sincere friend,
E. F. BENSON.

P. S.—I apologise for what I have said about your superficialness. It is, however, perfectly true.

I
To Introduce

The time has come, the showman said,
To look at many things,
At Deans and tea and men and Babes
At Cambridge and at King's.
Light-blue Lyrics.

"And I maintain," said Reggie, flourishing the Britannia-metal teapot (in order, it is supposed, to lend a spurious emphasis to the *banalité* of his sentiment), "that it's better to have played and lost than never—"

The teapot—one of those in which the handle is invariably the hottest part—had just been filled up with boiling water, and a clear and fervid amber stream flew bounteously out of its spout on to the bare knees of one of those who had played and lost. Thereupon a confused noise arose, and Reggie's sentence has never been finished.

After a short but violent interlude, the confused noise ceased by tacit consent, as suddenly as it had begun; Ealing helped Reggie to pick up the broken fragments that remained, and the latter had to drink his tea out of a pint glass.

"To think that a mere game of football should lead to such disastrous consequences," he remarked. "Why does tea out of a glass taste like hot Gregory powder?"

"I never drank hot Gregory powder; what does it taste like?"

"Why, like tea out of a glass," said Reggie brilliantly.

"Reggie, if you want to rag again, you've only got to say so."

Ealing threw into a corner the napkin with which he had been drying his knees and stocking after the tea-deluge, and as he had finished, took out a pipe, and proceeded to fill it.

"That pig of a half-back caught me a frightful hack on the shin," he said.

"Well, you kicked him in the stomach later on," said Reggie consolingly. "That's always something to fall back on. Besides he did it by accident, and it certainly looked as if you did it on purpose. Of course it may only have been sheer clumsiness."

"Dry up. You didn't funk as much as usual this afternoon."

"I tried to, but I never had time. And I can funk as quickly as any man in England. Jack, it's time for you to say something."

Jack Marsden was the only one of the three who looked in the least like a gentleman at that moment. Ealing and Reggie were both in change, they both wore villainously muddy flannel knickerbockers, short enough to disclose villainously muddy knees, old blazers, and strong, useful, football boots with bars. Jack, who had taken no part in the confused noise, was sitting in a low chair reading *Alice in Wonderland*, and eating cake in the manner of a man who does not think about dinner.

"I wasn't asleep," he remarked. "I heard every word you fellows were saying."

"Dormouse," explained Ealing.

"Dormouse it is. Give me some more tea, Reggie."

"I call it so jolly sociable to read a book when you come to tea," remarked Reggie.

"So do I. Thanks. And another piece of cake."

"Football's a beastly game," said Ealing.

"Especially when one is beaten. Here we are out of the Cup ties in the first round, and what one is to do now I don't know. I can't think why people ever play football."

"I shall work," said Ealing. "Have you seen the list of the subjects for the Mays? I think it must be meant for a joke. They have set all the classical authors I ever heard of, and nearly all I haven't ever heard of."

"I want a clean cup," quoted Jack.

"You want a clean—" began Reggie slowly in a tone of virulent condemnation. But being unable to finish his sentence in an adequately insulting manner, he left Jack's deficiencies to the imagination.

"He wants a clean pipe," remarked Ealing. "It sounds like a kettle boiling."

Jack shut up his book and yawned.

"You fellows are beastly funny," he said. "I'm going back to Trinity to work. For why? I am dining with the Babe to-night."

"The Babe has got markedly madder and several years younger since last term," said Ealing. "And he was neither sane nor old to begin with. Tell him so with my love. Or I dare say Reggie and I will come round later."

"Do. It is November the fifth. The Babe observes all feasts, whether civil or ecclesiastical. He says it would be a thousand pities to let these curious old customs lapse into disuse."

"I wish the Babe wouldn't use such beautiful language," said Ealing.

"He only does it in his less lucid intervals. Good-bye. I'll tell him you're coming round about ten."

Jack picked up his hat and stick and went off to his rooms in Trinity, where till half-past seven he drifted helplessly about like a ship-wrecked mariner, to whom no sail breaks the limitless horizon, in Thucydides's graphic account of the Peloponnesian war. To Jack, however, it appeared that its chief characteristic was its length, rather than its interest, a criticism, the truth of which is rendered more and more probable every year by an enormous mass of perfectly independent, unbiassed critics. But being a short and stout young man, by no means infirm of purpose, he regarded that merely as a reason the more for beginning at once.

Reggie Bristow and Ealing sat on for an hour or so by the fire. They were old friends, and so they did not need to talk much. Reggie was a year the younger of the two, and he was now half-way through his first term at King's. They had been at Eton five years together, where they had both extracted a good deal of amusement out of life, and perhaps a little profit. They were both exceedingly healthy, to judge by the superficial standards of examinations, rather stupid, and, in the opinion of those who knew them, on a much more important matter, very liveable-with. Furthermore, they both played games rather well, and, as was right, neither of them ever troubled his head about abstract questions of any sort or kind. Living was pleasant, and they proceeded to live.

Reggie had been performing this precarious feat with admirable steadiness for just nineteen years. Nature had gifted him with a pleasant face, and a healthy appetite had enabled him to show it to eminent advantage on the top of a tall body. He preferred talking to working, cricket to football, and lying in bed to "signing in" at 8 A.M. in the morning. He smoked a good many pipes every day, and blew smoke rings creditably. He played the piano a little, but his friends did not encourage him to take the necessary practice whereby he might play it any better. He was in fact perfectly normal, which is always the best thing to be.

"It's a great bore, our being beaten," he said, after a long pause, during which he had succeeded in blowing one smoke ring through another. "We were the best side really."

"Of course we were, although we are blessed with a goal-keeper who hides behind the goal-posts, until a man has had his shot."

"He stopped rather a hot one to-day."

"Purely by accident. He peeped out from the goal-post too soon, and it struck him in the stomach. I hate being beaten by Pemmer, though I shouldn't have minded if we'd lost to Trinity. The ground was in a filthy state too. One couldn't get off."

Reggie sighed.

"I've got to write to my father to-morrow," he said, "and tell him my impressions of Cambridge. It will be a little difficult, because I haven't got any."

"Of course you haven't. Only people in books have impressions. Describe the match to-day."

"I'm afraid it wouldn't interest him."

"Well, describe King's Chapel."

"I might do that; perhaps he's forgotten what it is like. Oh, yes, and I might describe some of the dons. I'm expected to be very earnest, you know, and the worst of it is I don't know how."

"Do you suppose one will ever become a responsible being?" asked Ealing.

"No, never," said Reggie emphatically. "I grow sillier and sillier every day."

"Well, you can't get much sillier."

Reggie shook his head.

"You wait a year or two," he said. "I don't suppose you can form the slightest impression of how foolish I can be if I like."

"What are you going to do when you go down?"

"The Lord knows," said Reggie. "I was considered remarkably bright for my age at one time."

"Long ago?"

"Ages ago. I don't suppose I've been considered bright for the last six years. Oh, by the way, they've put me into the Pitt."

"How very imprudent of them!"

"Yes. There was a young man in the Pitt."

"Well?"

"That's all. It's me, you know."

Ealing got up and stretched slowly and luxuriously.

"I must go and change. I believe one oughtn't to sit in wet things. But if one does it frequently enough, it doesn't seem to hurt one, and the same remark applies to muffins."

"I shall try sitting in a muffin," said Reggie thoughtfully. "I never thought of it before."

"Do. Are you going into Hall to-night?"

"Yes, unless you ask me to dinner."

"I have no intention whatever of doing that," said Ealing.

"Then we'll both go into Hall. I propose to drink champagne out of a silver mug to make up for the tea out of a glass."

"'Not what I wish but what I want,' as the Babe said the other day when he ordered six pairs of silk pyjamas."

"Oh, the Babe has his points," said Reggie.

Reggie's rooms looked out on to a small court, bounded on two sides by the new college buildings, on one by that pellucid river, from which, as Wordsworth might have said, "Cambridge has borrowed its name," and on the other by four or five big elm-trees. Beyond these lay the back lawn, growing a little rank just now with autumn rains, and above that the main buildings of the college, and the Chapel, which is quite worth describing even to the length of four sides of that smaller size of note-paper, which is found so eminently convenient a basis for the purpose of writing letters to relations.

His two rooms were on the third floor, opening the one into the other, and like all college rooms, were very thoughtfully supplied with an outer door which could only be opened from the inside, and by means of which the laborious student can shut himself off from sight and sound of the busy world around. During Reggie's short stay at Cambridge it had, as far as he knew, only been used once, and on that occasion a playful friend, mistaking its real use, had shut him out, having previously ascertained that he had lost the key. This feat has at least the merit of simplicity, and it appears to lose none of its fascination however constantly repeated.

Inside, they were furnished with a small bookcase, occupied by débutant-looking classical books, several low chairs, which may best be described as rather groggy, and had been taken on from the previous owner at a high valuation, a piano of a harsh and astringent quality of tone, but plenty of it, several high chairs, and two tables. The smaller of these Reggie preferred to call his working table, the only explanation of which seemed to lie in the fact that somebody often sat on the edge of it when the chairs were full. Two or three school groups and a couple of engravings hung on the walls, and the chimney-piece was littered with things which reminded one of the delightfully vague word "remnants," and consisted of candlesticks, pipes, old letters, loose matches, an ash tray, a clock which for the last month had been under the delusion that it was always ten minutes to four, an invitation to play in the Freshman's football match, and another to see the Dean at five minutes to seven, a watch and watch-chain, sixpence, a lawn-tennis ball, a small wooden doll in hideous nakedness (no explanation forthcoming), a pen, and a cigarette.

It was a cold evening, and Reggie wandered in and out of his bedroom, in a state of betwixt and between, now clad only in a bath towel, later on in a pair of trousers and socks, in the fulness of time completely clothed. It still wanted five or ten minutes to seven, and he stood in front of the fire warming himself till Hall time, feeling in that deliciously half-tired, half-lazy mood which is the inimitable result of violent exercise. He rummaged aimlessly in the débris on the mantel-piece, and suffering the deserved fate of idle hands, found the Dean's note about which he had genuinely forgotten. He gave vent to a resigned little sound, about half-way between a sigh and a swear, took up his gown and left the room.

II
In Fellows' Buildings

King, nine, twa, do you play them so?
Whae's that a-calling?
I dinna ken, and I do not know
Whae's that a-calling sae sweet.
On the Border.

And one clear call for me.
Tennyson.

Those Fellows of colleges, who live in college are, for obvious reasons, debarred from the matrimonial state, and should inspire greater respect in reflective minds than almost any other class of persons in this naughty world. For the most part they combine the morality of married men with the innocence of ideal bachelors. Their lives are for nine months or so of the year lived in the sequestered shades of pious and ancient foundations, unspotted by the world. Those who have relations fill their places in the domestic circle where their absence has no doubt rendered them doubly dear, at Christmas and Easter, or join those who have not, and pass their long vacation on the lower slopes of the Alps, or at quiet little sea-side places; some of them visit cathedrals during their unoccupied months, some the lakes, few or none, London, or if London, chiefly the reading-room at the British Museum. But there are exceptions to the most desirable rules, and even among Fellows of colleges there are a few who are reported to know "a thing or two."

On Saturday night it often happened that Fellows of King's asked their colleagues from other colleges to dine with them. After dinner they sat in the Combination Room for an hour or so, or they would break up into parties, which spent the evening at one or other of the Fellows' rooms, and indulged in the mild dissipation of whist at three-penny points, which they seemed to find strangely exhilarating. One such party adjourned directly after dinner to the room of the Dean, Mr. Collins, who two hours before had remonstrated with Reggie for not attending a larger percentage of early Chapels or their equivalent. To undergraduates he was scholastic and austere, but among his own contemporaries he not infrequently relaxed into positive playfulness.

Mr. Stewart, a history tutor from Trinity, was one of his guests to-night, and Mr. Longridge, a Dean of the same college, another. About Mr. Longridge, all that need be said at present is that in body he was insignificant, and in mind, incoherent. But Mr. Stewart was a more conspicuous person both bodily and mentally: he was in fact one of the exceptions to the general run of his class, and he was credited, by report at least, with knowing not only a thing or two, but lots of things.

Just now, his long, languid form, attired altogether elegantly, was spread over a considerable area of arm-chair, his feet rested on the fender, and he was holding forth on certain subjects of the day, about which he was perfectly qualified to speak. The man with the incoherent mind was sitting near him, listening with ill-concealed impatience to his sonorous periods, and getting in a word edgewise occasionally. Mr. Collins was busy attending to the wants of his guests, and two of his friends from the same college, were sitting together on the sofa, resigned but replete.

"The luxury of modern times," Mr. Stewart was saying, "is disgusting,—Chartreuse, please—simply disgusting. What business have men to clothe their floors in fabrics from Persia, their walls in other fabrics from Cairo and Algiers, or stamped leather, and paintings by Turner and Reynolds and, and Orchardson, their lamp-shades in lace and Liberty fabrics—Lace and Liberty sounds like a party catch-word—and leave their minds naked and unashamed? I myself aim at a studious simplicity—Thank you, I have brought my own cigarettes. Won't you have one? They are straight from Constantinople—a studious simplicity. I live at Cambridge, while my natural sphere is London and Paris. I get up at seven, while nature bids me stay in bed till ten. I—"

Mr. Longridge could not bear it any longer. He sprang out of his chair as a cuckoo flies out of a cuckoo clock on the stroke of the hour, and adjusted his spectacles.

"Well, take the case of a man who, say, lived at Oxford. Supposing—or well, take another case—"

Mr. Stewart took advantage of a momentary pause to continue.

"Yes, of course, very interesting," he said. "A delightful town, Oxford. A shadow of the romance of mediævalism still lingers about its grey streets, which is quite absent from the new red-brick buildings of St. John's College, Cambridge. I remember walking there one morning with dear George Meredith, and your mention of Oxford recalled to me what he said. Poor dear fellow! He is the most lucid of men, but as soon as he puts pen to paper he is like an elephant that is lost in a jungle, and goes trumpeting and trampling along through wreaths and tangled festoons of an exotic style. Lord Granchester was staying there at the time—Sir Reginald Bristow he was then—"

"I had the pleasure of speaking to his son just before Hall," remarked Mr. Stewart in professional accents.

"Reggie, is dear Reggie up here? How delightful! I remember him six or seven years ago. He was like one of Raphael's angels."

"What-was-it-that-George-Meredith-said?" asked the incoherent man, all in one word.

"One of Raphael's angels," pursued Mr. Stewart, taking not the slightest notice. "A face like an opening flower."

"The flower has a stem six feet high now," remarked Mr. Collins.

"Dear Reggie! And—and is he as fascinating as ever?"

Mr. Collins laughed.

"I have not known him long, so I cannot say how fascinating he is capable of being. And as a rule Deans and undergraduates don't put out their full power of fascination in dealing with each other."

"But whose fault is that?" said Mr. Stewart in a slow unctuous voice. "Surely we ought to be brothers, dear elder brothers to the undergraduates. I remember—"

Mr. Collins, who was obviously sceptical about George Meredith's remark, and hoped that Stewart was going back to it, brightened up and interrogated, "Yes?" in an intelligent manner.

"I remember," said Mr. Stewart still sublimely oblivious, "I remember that I myself used always to make friends, dear friends of the undergraduates when I was Dean. If one of them did not attend Chapel often enough, as often, that is, as our odious regulations require, I used to ask him to call for me on his way, and we used to go to Chapel together. One had a rich, lovely tenor voice. I—I forget his name, and I think he is dead."

Mr. Longridge laughed monosyllabically but unkindly.

"It was very pleasant, very pleasant indeed, but to be Dean brings one into the wrong relation with undergraduates," said Mr. Stewart. "And talking of music, I had a charming time at Bayreuth last year. We had *Parsifal* and *Tannhäuser* and the *Meistersingers*. *Tannhäuser* is the most wonderful creation. Like all of us, but more successfully than most, Wagner welds into one harmonious whole, the ugliness of sin and the beauty of holiness."

Mr. Longridge—there is no other word—bridled.

"The beauty of holiness," continued Mr. Stewart, chewing and masticating his words, so as to get the full flavour out of them, "a human soul capable of anything. Venusberg and Rome are alike interludes to him. He goes on his sublimely humorous way from Venusberg to Elizabeth, from Elizabeth to Venusberg, and neither produces any lasting effect. And how supremely natural the end is! He has left an almond rod at Rome, and because one of the pilgrims, one of a dowdy crew of middle-class pilgrims shows him an almond rod in blossom, he rushes to the conclusion that it is his. How illogical, but how natural! And he who has never had the courage of his opinions either at Venusberg or Rome, is 'struck of a heap,' as they say in suburban places, by the flowering almond rod, and instantly gives up the ghost. Maskelyne and Cooke could produce a bundle of flowering almond rods in half the time. We pay five shillings to see them all. Tannhäuser paid his life to see one. He died of joy at the sight of that flowering almond rod. And after all it was only artificial flowers twined round a stick."

"Well, of course, if you choose to look at it in that way," ejaculated Mr. Longridge.

"My dear Longridge," said Mr. Stewart very slowly, "there is only one way to look at things, only one way."

"Not at all, though you might very fairly say that there was only one man to look at in one way. *Quot homines, tot sententiæ.*"

"Dear old Longridge," said Stewart with unctuous affection.

"You might just as well say," continued Mr. Longridge, "that because there are people who are colour-blind, we none of us know green from red."

There was perhaps nothing in the world which Mr. Longridge enjoyed so heartily as what he called a good, sharp argument. This usually consisted in his putting forward a great quantity of indefensible and irrelevant propositions himself, and then proceeding to show how indefensible they were: their irrelevancy needed no demonstration. He was a man of mixed mind.

"Dear old Longridge," repeated Stewart. "Some people have the misfortune to be born colour-blind, and no doubt in the next world they will be extraordinarily keen-sighted. But until we have finished with this world, and I have not, we can leave colour-blind people altogether out of the question, can we not? In fact, I don't know how they found their way in. Some things are green, others red, and if you call them by their wrong names, even your own friends must allow that you are no judge of colour."

Mr. Longridge who was very near-sighted, seemed disposed to take this personally.

"But because I differ from you, *in toto* I may say, that is no proof that I am colour-blind. You might just as well say—well, to take another instance—"

"To take another instance," said Mr. Stewart, "because you are sleepy, that is no reason why I should go to bed. In fact, I will have just a glass more of Chartreuse. What a lovely colour it is. A decadent, abnormal colour, the colour of a spoiled piece of soul-fabric. Yes, quite delicious. I spent a fortnight once in the monastery at Fécamp, full of dear, delightful, ascetic monks. I think they all put boiled peas in their shoes during the day, which must be horribly squashy, but they all drink Chartreuse after dinner, so they end happily. Dear, impossible Charles Kingsley used always to abuse monks—I suppose because he was tinged with asceticism himself. But I fancy there is no real objection to their marrying. Monks marry nuns, I think. How delightful to receive an invitation card—'Monk and Nun Stewart.'"

The two other Fellows of King's had subsided into the background altogether, and were discussing the chances of their various pupils in the next tripos. They had both refused Chartreuse, and took their coffee in a mixture of half and half with hot milk. The integral calculus on one side balanced an exceptional skill at Greek Iambics on the other, and they prattled on politely and innocently. It must be conceded that they felt but little interest in what they were talking about, but their interest on all subjects was diminutive and bird-like. They pecked and hopped away.

"But he showed me a copy of Iambics the other day," said one, "with two final Cretics in it."

Mr. Stewart caught the last words.

"What an epigram that ought to make!" he said, smiling broadly and benignly. "The insidious and final Cretic. I see him as a lean, spare man, with a cast in his eye."

"It's merely a false foot in Greek Iambics they are talking of," said Longridge breathlessly.

"And a false foot," continued Stewart, "cunningly concealed by patent leather boots. Thank you, Longridge, the picture is complete. And I have a Victor Hugo class in my room at half-past ten. We are reading *Les Misérables*—a—a prose epic. I must literally be going."

"I should like to see a figurative going," said Mr. Longridge, spitefully.

Mr. Stewart turned on him with mild forbearance.

"You can say you must be going and then stop," he said. "Good night, good night. A most pleasant evening."

There were now only four of them, so at their host's proposal they settled down to whist. Mr. Longridge enquired eagerly whether it was to be long whist or short whist, but as no one had ever heard of either, it is to be presumed that they played medium, and it is certain they played mediocre whist. Mr. Longridge during the first deal, demonstrated quite conclusively that whist markers could be used either for whist or backgammon or bézique, always supposing you knew how to multiply by ten, or with somewhat less ease for registering the votes in the present election. This latter, however, appeared, as far as it was possible to follow him, to imply a knowledge of how to multiply by thirteen and divide by twenty-nine, a feat which all his hearers, with the exception of the mathematician, were hopelessly incapable of performing. This, however, was no detraction whatever from the abstract value of such a discovery.

Longridge was partner to Mr. Campbell, one of the hitherto silent guests, and Collins to Currey, who was cursed with the final Cretic pupil. And herein lay the sting of the affair, for Longridge's studies in whist had got as far as the call for trumps, while his partner's knowledge was confined to a complete acquaintance with the ordinal value of individual cards. Collins, however, was a sound player, and the only one present, excepting Longridge, who knew what a call for trumps meant. Longridge consequently stripped his hand naked, as it were, for the sole benefit of his adversary. The rest were as Teiresias, struck blind by the sight of five trumps unveiled.

With his habitual acumen the Dean of Trinity perceived this during the second rubber, and without communicating his discovery, as he was strongly tempted to do, played the higher of two cards instead of the lower so persistently in the first round, in order to deceive his adversary on the right, that before the game was three deals old he had irrevocably revoked. Holding the knave and nine of clubs he played the higher of the two on to the queen third hand, and deceived by his own acuteness supposed he had no more, and trumped the second round. Whereby his adversaries went out, a treble.

Reggie and Ealing, meantime, had spent a charming evening. Reggie had been pressed not to play the piano after Hall, and, instead, they had played billiards till just before ten, and then gone round to Malcolm Street to come down to dessert at the Babe's dinner party.

As it was Guy Fawkes's day, their course, so to speak, was mapped out for them beyond possibility of error, and Reggie had the prospect of being exactly six shillings and eight-pence poorer than he otherwise would have been, at about 10.30 on Monday morning.

III
The Babe

O bitter world, where one who longs
To be recorded unforgiven,
Bewitched and wild, is called a child
Fit to be seen in any heaven.
Hotchpotch Verses.

The Babe was a cynical old gentleman of twenty years of age, who played the banjo charmingly. In his less genial moments he spoke querulously of the monotony of the services of the Church of England, and of the hopeless respectability of M. Zola. His particular forte was dinner parties for six, skirt dancing and acting, and the performances of the duties of half-back at Rugby football. His dinner parties were selected with the utmost carelessness, his usual plan being to ask the first five people he met, provided he did not know them too intimately. With a wig of fair hair, hardly any rouge, and an ingénue dress, he was the image of Vesta Collins, and that graceful young lady might have practised before him, as before a mirror. But far the most remarkable point about the Babe, considering his outward appearance and other tastes, was his brilliance as a Rugby football player. He was extraordinarily quick with the ball, his passing was like a beautiful dream, and he dodged, as was universally known, like the devil. It was a sight for sore eyes to see the seraphic, smooth-faced Babe waltzing gaily about among rough-bearded barbarians, pretending to pass and doing nothing of the kind, dropping neatly out of what looked like the middle of the scrimmage, or flickering about in a crowd which seemed to be unable to touch him with a finger.

Last night the Babe had been completely in his element. His dinner party consisted of a rowing-blue, a man who had been sent down from Oxford, a Dean who was to preach the University sermon next day, and was the Babe's uncle, Jack Marsden, a gentleman from Corpus, who had a very rosy chance, so said his friends, of representing Cambridge against Oxford at chess, and himself. Later on, Reggie and Ealing had come in, who with the help of the rowing man broke both his sofas; the gentleman from

Oxford had insisted, to the obvious discomfort of the Dean, on talking to him about predestination, a subject of which the Dean seemed to know nothing whatever; the chess-man had played bézique with Jack, and the Babe had presided over them all with infantine cynicism. A little later on, when the Dean had gone away, he had danced a skirt-dance in a sheet and a night-gown, and they ended up the evening by what the Babe called "a set piece" from his window, consisting of a catherine wheel, and four Roman candles, not counting the rocket which exploded backwards through the Babe's chandelier, narrowly missing the head of the man from Corpus, whose chance of getting his chess-blue would, if it had hit, have been totally extinguished. In order to lend verisimilitude to the proceedings Reggie had gone into the street and called "Oh-h-h-h," at intervals, and as he had left his cap and gown in the Babe's room, he was very promptly and properly proctorised.

The Babe breakfasted next morning at the civilised hour of ten, and observed with a faint smile that the rocket stick was deeply imbedded in the ceiling, and he ate his eggs and bacon with a serene sense of the successful incongruity of his little party the night before. The gentleman from Oxford who was staying with him had not yet appeared, but the Babe waited for no man, when he was hungry.

The furniture of his rooms was as various and as diverse as his accomplishments. Several of Mr. Aubrey Beardsley's illustrations from the Yellow Book, clustering round a large photograph of Botticelli's Primavera, which the Babe had never seen, hung above one of the broken sofas, and in his bookcase several numbers of the Yellow Book, which the Babe declared bitterly had turned grey in a single night, since the former artist had ceased to draw for it, were ranged side by side with Butler's *Analogies*, Mr. Sponge's *Sporting Tour*, and Miss Marie Corelli's *Barabbas*. It is, however, only fair to the Babe to say that Bishop Butler's volume had been part of the "set piece" for his Littlego, and that he referred to Miss Corelli as the arch humourist of English literature. A pair of dumb-bells, each weighing fifty-six pounds, stood by the fireplace, but these the Babe had never been known to use in order to further his muscular development; he only rolled them over the floor with the patient look of one who had the destinies of the world on his shoulders, whenever the lodger below played the piano. It may be remarked that the two were not on speaking terms.

"And herein," said the Babe, when he explained the use of the dumb-bells the evening before, "herein lies half the bitterness of human life."

He was pressed to explain further, but only replied sadly,

"So near and yet so far," and showed how it was possible to imitate the experience of a sea-sick passenger on the channel, by means of "that simple, and I may add, delicious fruit, the common orange."

It was a most realistic and spirited performance, and all that the Dean could do was to ejaculate feebly, "Do stop, Babe," between his spasms of laughter.

The Babe had finished his breakfast, which he ate with a good appetite, heartily, before the gentleman from Oxford appeared, and proceeded to skim the *Sunday Times*. When he did appear he looked a little disconsolately at the breakfast table, and lifting up a dish-cover found some cold bacon, at which he blanched visibly, and demanded soda water.

"What did you eat for breakfast, Babe?" he asked.

The Babe looked up apologetically.

"I'm afraid I ate all the eggs, and the bacon must be cold by now," he said. "But I'll send for some more."

"No thanks. Where's the tea?"

The Babe rang the bell.

"It'll be here in a moment. I drank cocoa."

Leamington finished his soda water, and sat down.

"There is no end to your greatness. Cocoa! Great Scot! My tongue is the colour of mortar."

"I'm so sorry. I feel quite well, thanks. Will you have some Eno's fruit salts? I know my landlady's got some, because she offered me them the other day when I had a cold. Here's your tea. Do you ever read the Pink 'un? It's funny without being prudish."

Leamington poured out some tea.

"Don't read, Babe; it's unsociable. Talk to me while I eat."

The Babe put down the current copy of the *Sunday Times*, and laid himself out to be pleasant.

"There are some people coming to lunch at two," he said. "I rather think I asked Reggie. Poor Reggie, he got dropped on in a minute by the Proggins. Oh, yes, and so is Stewart. Do you know Stewart? He's a don at Trinity, and is supposed to be wicked. I wish someone would suppose me to be wicked. But I'm beginning to be afraid they never will."

"You must lose your look of injured innocence or rather cultivate the injury at the expense of the innocence. Grow a moustache; no one looks battered and world-weary without a moustache."

"I can't. I bought some Allen's Hair Restorer the other day, but it only smarted. I wonder if they made a mistake and gave me Allen's Antifat?"

"You don't look as if they had," said Leamington, "at least it doesn't look as if it had had much effect. Wouldn't it take?"

"Not a bit," said the Babe. "I applied it night and morning to my upper lip, and it only smelt and smarted. I suppose you can't restore a thing that has never existed. I think I shall be a clergyman, because all clergymen cut their moustaches off, and to do that you must have one."

"I see. But isn't that rather elaborate?"

"No means are elaborate if you desire the end enough," said the Babe sententiously. "I shall marry too, because married people are bald, and I'm sure I don't wonder."

"So are babies."

"Not in the same way, and don't be personal. I can't think of any other means of losing the appearance of innocence. Suggest some: you've been rusticated."

"Why don't you—"

"I've tried that, and it's no use."

"But you don't know what I was going to say," objected Leamington.

"I know I don't. But I've tried it," said the wicked Babe. "I've even read the Yellow Book through from cover to cover, and as you see, framed the pictures by Aubrey Beardsley. The Yellow Book is said to add twenty years per volume to any one's life. Not at all. It has left me precisely where it found me, whereas, according to that, as I've read five volumes, I ought to be, let's see—five times twenty, plus twenty—a hundred and twenty. I don't look it, you know. It's no use your telling me I do, because I don't. I have no illusions whatever about the matter."

"I wasn't going to tell you anything of the kind," said Leamington. "But you should take yourself more seriously. I believe that is very aging."

The Babe opened his eyes in the wildest astonishment.

"Why I take myself like Gospels and Epistles," he said. "The fault is that no one else takes me seriously. You would hardly believe," he continued with some warmth, "that the other night I was proctorised, and that when the Proctor saw who I was—he's a Trinity man—he said, 'Oh, it's only you. Go home at once, Babe.' It is perfectly disheartening. I offered to let him search me to see whether I had such a thing as a cap or a gown concealed anywhere about me. And the bull-dogs grinned. How can I be a devil of a fellow, if I'm treated like that?"

"I should have thought a Rugby blue could have insisted on being treated properly."

"No, that's all part of the joke," shrieked the infuriated Babe. "It's supposed to add a relish to the silly pointless joke of treating me like a child and calling me 'Babe.' I've never been called anything but Babe since I can remember. And when I try to be proctorised the very bull-dogs come about me, making mouths at me."

"Rough luck. Try it on again."

"It's a pure waste of time," said the Babe disconsolately. "I might go out for a drive with all the bed-makers of this college in a tandem, and no one would take the slightest notice of me. Besides I can never make a tandem go straight. The leader always turns round and winks at me. It knows perfectly well that I'm only the Babe, bless its heart. I edited a perfectly scandalous magazine here last term you know, every day during the May week. It simply teemed with scurrilous suggestiveness. It insulted directly every one with whom I was acquainted, and many people with whom I was not. It compared the Vice-Chancellor to an old toothbrush, and drew a trenchant parallel between the Proctors and the town drainage. It suggested that the antechapel of King's should be turned into a shooting-gallery, and the side chapels into billiard-rooms. It proposed that I should be appointed Master of Magdalen, I forget why at this moment. It contained the results of a *plébiscite* as to who should be Vice-Chancellor for the next year, and the under-porter of King's got in easily, with Jack Marsden as a bad second. It proposed the substitution of dominoes and hopscotch—I haven't the least idea what hopscotch is, but it sounds to me simply obscene—for the inter-university contests at cricket and rowing. And that magazine," said the Babe dramatically, rising from his chair, and addressing Primavera, "that magazine was welcomed, welcomed, Madam, by all classes. The innocent lambs, whose reputation I ought to have ruined came bleating after me and said how they had enjoyed it. It sold by hundreds, when it ought to have been suppressed: people thought it funny, whereas it was only hopelessly foolish and vulgar, though I say it who shouldn't; while those few people who had the sense to see how despicable the whole production really was, told each other that 'it was only Me.' Me! I'm almost sick of the word. I was put 'in Authority' in the Granta, when I ought to have been sent down—The Vice-Chancellor asked me to dinner on the very day when I published a most infernal and libellous lampoon about him, and I have already told you how the Proctors treat me. It is enough," said the Babe in conclusion, "to make one take the veil, I mean the tonsure, and dry up the milk of human kindness within one."

"Hear, hear," shouted Leamington. "Good old Babe."

The Babe glared at him a moment, with wide, indignant eyes and then went on rather shrilly:

"Look at Reggie. I'm older than he is, at least I think so, and any one with a grain of sense would say that I therefore ought to know better, and what is excusable in him, is not excusable in me, but he goes and says 'Oh' in the street and he is treated as a dangerous character, sent home, and will be fined. I might say 'Oh' till Oscar Browning got into Parliament, and do you suppose they would ever consider me a dangerous character? Not they. (Here the Babe laughed in a hollow and scornful manner.) They would treat me with that infernal familiarity which I so deprecate, and say, 'Go home, Babe.' Babe indeed!"

The Babe's voice broke, and he flung himself into his chair after the manner of Sarah Bernhardt, and hissed out *"Misérables! Comme je les déteste!"*

Leamington applauded this histrionic effort, and feeling a little better after breakfast, lit a cigarette. The maidservant came to clear breakfast away, and as she left the room the Babe resumed in the gentle, melancholy tones, which were natural to him:

"If I thought it would do any good, I would go and snatch a kiss from that horrid, rat-faced girl as she is carrying the tray down stairs. But it wouldn't, you know; it wouldn't do any good at all. She wouldn't complain to the landlady, or if she did it would only end in my giving her half-a-crown. Besides, I don't in the least want to kiss her—I wouldn't do it if she gave me half-a-crown. I wonder what George Moore would do if he were me. We'll ask Stewart when he comes to lunch. He is intimate with all notable people. George Moore is notable isn't he? I fancy W. H. Smith & Son boycotted him. Stewart said the other day that the Emperor of Germany was one of the nicest emperors he had ever seen."

"That's nothing," said Leamington. "There's a don at Oxford who has written a book called *Princes I have Persecuted without Encouragement.*"

The Babe laughed.

"A companion volume to Stewart's *Monarchs I have Met*. Not that he has written such a book. Stewart is perfectly charming, but he thinks a lot of a Prince. If he hasn't written *Monarchs I have Met*, he ought to have."

"We all ought to have done a lot of things we haven't done," said Leamington.

"We had a butler once," said the Babe, "who never would say the General Confession, because he said he hadn't left undone the things he ought to have done, and it went against his conscience to say he had. He got the sack soon after for leaving the door of the cellar undone, and for getting drunk."

"So he was undone himself."

"When I grow up," said the Babe with less bitterness, but returning like a burned moth to the sore subject—no charge for mixed metaphors—"I shall live exclusively in the society of archdeacons. Perhaps they might think me wicked. Yet I don't know—my uncle whom you met last night thinks I'm such a good boy, and he's a dean."

"I doubt if they would. The other day some one sent a telegram to the Archdeacon of Basingstoke, a man of whom he knew nothing except that he was a teetotaller and an anti-vivisectionist, saying, 'Fly at once, all is discovered.' The Archdeacon flew, and has never been heard of since. No one has the slightest idea where he has gone or what he had done. You know you wouldn't fly, Babe, if you were sent telegrams like that by the hundred."

"How little you know me," said the Babe dramatically. "I should fly like fun. Don't you see if one flew, one's character for wickedness would be established beyond all doubt. I might send a telegram to myself, telling me to fly. Then I should fly, but leave the telegram lying about in a conspicuous position. After a year's absence I should return, but my character would be gone beyond all hopes of recovery, and the world would do me justice at last."

"Poor misunderstood Babe! Why don't you go to Oxford, saying you've been sent down from Cambridge? What time do we lunch?"

"Oh, about two, and it's half-past twelve already. Let's go round to the Pitt. This evening we will go to Trinity Chapel. A little walk is very wholesome after breakfast. Besides I shall go in a bowler, and perhaps we shall meet at Proggins. I shall insult him if we do."

IV
vs. Blackheath

For he was very fast,
And he ran and he passed,
And the sun and the moon and the stars
Tried to catch him by the tail,
But they one and all did fail,
And Venus broke her nose 'gainst Mars.
Hotchpotch Verses.

The Babe hurt his knee playing against the Old Leysians, and his language was Aristophanic and savoured strongly of faint praise. Also one of the Old Leysians had grossly insulted him during the course of the game. The Babe was careering about with the ball behind their touch-line, attempting to get a try straight behind the goal-posts, instead of being content with one a reasonable distance off, for he was fastidious in these little matters and liked to do things well, when he was caught up bodily by one of the opposing team and carried safely out into the field again. A roar of appreciative laughter, and shouts of "Good old Babe" went up from all the field, and the Babe's feelings were hurt. He had the satisfaction of dropping a goal a little later on, but he asked pathetically, "Could aught atone?"

Before "Time" was called he had hurt his knee, and as already mentioned he was Aristophanic for a few days.

The next match was against Blackheath, and the Babe had not yet recovered sufficiently to play. He had bought an Inverness cloak "so loud," he said, "that you could scarcely hear yourself speak," and a cross-eyed bull-pup, in order to dispel that universal but distressing illusion about his childishness, which so vexed his soul, and he was going to lunch with Reggie and look at the match afterwards. Bill Sykes, the bull-dog, was coming too, in order to be seen with the Babe by as many people as possible, and his master drove to King's gate with his Inverness and his bull-dog, and his seraphic smile, in the best of tempers. It was necessary to smuggle Mr. Sykes, as the Babe insisted that strangers should call him, through the court without his being seen, and the Babe hobbled along, still being rather lame, presenting a curious lopsided appearance which was caused by Mr. Sykes, who was tucked away beneath the Inverness. A confused growling sound issued at intervals from somewhere below his left arm, drowning even the loudness of the Inverness, and the Babe murmured encouragement and threats alternately. The porter stared suspiciously at this odd figure as it passed, but the serenity of the Babe's smile was as infinite as ever.

The Babe's hansom had been told to wait at the back gate of King's, but it had apparently found waiting tedious, and as there were no others about, they had to walk. Mr. Sykes, however, took this opportunity to behave, as the Babe said, "like the dog of a real blood," and had a delightful turn-up with a mongrel gentleman of his acquaintance, which did him much credit.

The game had not yet begun when they reached the Corpus ground, and both Sykes and the Babe's cloak can hardly have failed to be noticed. The Babe hobbled about among the two teams who were kicking about before the game began, and said it was much pleasanter looking on than playing, and that he meant to give it up, as it was a game more suited to savages than gentlemen. Two of the home team resented these remarks, and removed him, kindly but firmly, beyond the touch-line.

He and Reggie had secured chairs towards the centre of the ground, and it pleased the Babe to affect a childlike ignorance of everything connected with the rules and regulations of Rugby football, and he kept up a flow of fatuous remarks.

"Look how they are throwing the ball about! Why do they do that, Reggie? Which side is getting the best of it? Look at that funny little man with a flag, why do they all stop when he holds it up? I suppose it must be the captain. Have they got any try-downs yet, or do you call them touches? Oh, the ball's coming over here. I wish they'd take more care; it might easily have hit me. Why don't they have a better one? It's got all out of shape; it isn't a bit round. Mr. Sykes wants to play too. What a darling! Bite it then! How rough they are! Why did Hargreaves stamp on that man so?"

The effect of Hargreaves' "stamping on that man" was that he got the ball and a nice clear run. He was playing three quarters on the right, and when he got fairly off he was as fast as any man in England. His weak point, however, was starting: he could not start full speed as the Babe did, being heavy and a trifle clumsy. But he got twenty yards clear now, and making the most of it he was well off before the Blackheath team realised what was happening.

The Babe's fatuities died away as Hargreaves started and he stood silent a moment. It was clear that there was a good opening to hand, barring accidents. The game was close to the University twenty-five on the far side of the ground, and the Blackheath three-quarters were for the moment much too close to the scrimmage. It was impossible to get through even with the most finished passing on that side, and Hargreaves ran right across parallel to the goal disregarding the possibility of being collared in the centre of the ground opposite to the home goal, but trusting to his own speed. The outside Blackheath three-quarters came racing along, running slightly back in order to tackle him as he turned, but in a few moments it was clear that he was outpaced. Hargreaves ran clear round him as a yacht clears the buoy with a few yards to spare.

"Oh, well run," shouted the Babe. "Don't pass; get in yourself."

Hargreaves and the Blackheath back were now close to each other about the level of the Blackheath twenty-five, and nearly in the middle of the ground. The Varsity centre three-quarters had run straight up the ground while Hargreaves ran round, and was now in a position to be passed to again, but two Blackheath three-quarters were close to him. Then, by a fatal error, Hargreaves wavered a moment, instead of again trusting to his pace, got tackled, and in that moment of slack speed his own centre three-quarters got in front of him. He passed wildly and forward. An appeal, a whistle, a flag, and a free kick.

"Damn," said the Babe in a loud, angry voice.

The game flickered about between the two twenty-fives for the next ten minutes, going fast and loose, with a good deal of dribbling on the part of the forwards, and a corresponding amount of self-immolation on the part of the halves, who hurled themselves recklessly on the ball in the face of the fastest rushes, and seemed to the unaccustomed eye to be feverishly courting a swift and muddy death. Hargreaves made a few futile attempts to run through and failed egregiously.

Half-time was called shortly afterwards, neither team having scored. The Babe hobbled out into the field to make himself unpleasant to his side. Mr. Sykes followed, wheezing pathetically, and the Babe's Inverness cloak came in for renewed comments and reproof.

"They are weak on the outside," said the sage Babe to Hargreaves, "and a great man like you can run round as easy as perdition. You ought to stand much wider, and if you think you can get through the centre you are wrong. Stoddard could stop fifty of you. Good-bye."

The Blackheath team had come to the same conclusion as the Babe, and they kept the game tight. They had quite realised that the Varsity three-quarters on the left was weak, and that Hargreaves on the right was abominably fast. In consequence they did their best to screw the scrimmage round to Hargreaves' side, so as to hamper him by not leaving him room to get off. Time after time his half fed him persistently, and time after time he was unable to get round between the touch-line and the forwards. Meantime, the Blackheath pack, which were heavier and rather better together than Cambridge, were working their way slowly and steadily down the ground, keeping the ball close and comfortable among them. Hargreaves again and again, following the Babe's advice, stood right away on the left of the scrimmage when it approached the right touch-line, but his *vis-à-vis* as regularly stood close to him, and embraced him affectionately but roughly as soon as the ball got to him and before he had time to pass; but for the next quarter the game was very tight, and with the exception of a couple of free kicks given for offside play among the Blackheath forwards, the ball rarely left the scrimmage. Even these were returned by the back into touch, and the forwards settled down on the ball again like swarming bees.

The Babe, meantime, had been insolent to the referee, who was an old friend, and also an old hand. He had gone so far as to leave the game to take care of itself for a moment to tell the Babe candidly and in a loud, clear voice that he should be severely treated afterwards, adding as a further insult, "Of course we all know it's only you." The Babe was furious but impotent. The glory of the ulster and the bull-pup was entirely neutralised.

But he soon forgot these insolences; there were only ten minutes left, and neither side had scored more than minor points. To the unprofessional eye it seemed likely that they might go on playing for hours like this without either side scoring. The Blackheath forwards gained ground very slowly, but this was made up for with tiresome monotony by the quick punting of the University halves whenever they got the chance. The three-quarters stood and shivered, and the University back declared bitterly and audibly that he might as well have stopped at home.

But the professional Babe knew better. If once the ball came fairly out, the three-quarters would have a look in, and for himself he placed his money on Hargreaves. And in defiance of law, order, and decorum he shouted his advice to the half who was playing substitute for him.

"Don't punt," he shouted, "but pass."

The half at that moment was busy punting, and the Babe repeated his advice. Two minutes afterwards the half took it, as an exceptional opportunity presented itself, and passed to his centre three-quarters, and the Babe stood on his chair. Centre ran a short way and passed to the left, who passed back to centre, and centre to right. It was as pretty a piece of passing as one would wish to see on a winter's day.

This was the moment for which the Babe was waiting. The field was broken up and Hargreaves had the ball. He ran: they all ran. He ran fastest—there is nothing like simple language for epical events. He got a try which was not converted into a goal. But as no other points were scored, Cambridge won the match by one point to *nil*.

The Babe and Mr. Sykes went back to take their tea with Reggie, and Ealing who had been playing the Eton game, joined them. The Babe ate three muffins with a rapt air, and Mr. Sykes drank his tea out of the slop-basin like a Christian. He took cream and three lumps of sugar. His idea of how to eat muffins was a little sketchy, but otherwise be behaved charmingly. But, as the Babe said, to put pieces of half-masticated muffin on the carpet while you drink your tea, is a thing seldom, if ever, done in the best houses.

Ealing himself eschewed muffin on the ground of its being "bad training," and the Babe, who held peculiar views on training, proceeded to express them.

"One does every thing best," he said, "when one is most content. Personally I am most content when I have eaten a large lunch. Nobody could play Rugger in the morning. Why? Simply because no one is in a good temper in the morning, except those under-vitalised people who are never in a bad one, and who also never play games. Of course after a very large lunch one cannot run quite so fast, but one is serene, and serenity has much more to do with winning a match than pace. Yes, another cup of tea, please. Now Hargreaves is most content when he has had a little bread and marmalade and water. Every one to his taste. I hate water except when it's a hot bath. Water is meant not to drink, but to heat and wash in."

"Babe, do you mean to say you have hot baths in the morning?"

"Invariably when the weather is cold, and a cigarette, whatever the weather is. I am no Charles Kingsley, though I used to collect butterflies when I was a child."

"But when you became a Babe, you put away childish things," suggested Ealing.

A malignant light beamed from the Babe's eye.

"I ask you: do Babes have bull-pups?"

"I know one who has. I daresay he's an exception, though."

"When I was at a private school," remarked the Babe severely, "and a chap said a thing like that, we used to call him a funny ass."

Reggie shouted.

"Good old Babe. Has the referee caught you yet? He belongs to this college, and he may be in any minute. In fact, I asked him to come to tea. I don't know why he hasn't."

"If you want me to go, say so," said the Babe.

"Not a bit of it. It was only for your sake I suggested it. Smoke."

The Babe was limping about the room and came upon a set of chessmen.

"I want to play chess," he said. "Chess is the most delightful game if you treat it as a game of pure chance. You ought to move your queen into the middle of the board and then see what happens. To reduce it to the level of a sum in advanced mathematics, is a scandal and an outrage. To calculate the effect of a move takes away all the excitement."

"You may always calculate it wrong."

"In that case it becomes a nuisance. Reggie, will you play?"

"No."

"Ealing?"

"I can't. I don't know the moves."

"Nor do I. We should be about equal. Supposing you set two Heathen Chinese to play chess, which would win?"

"Is it a riddle?"

The Babe sank down again in his chair.

"I don't know," he said. "If it is, I give up. By the way what are you two chaps doing to-morrow?"

"Stop in bed till ten," said Reggie, "it being the Day of Rest: Chapel. Breakfast. Lunch. Pitt. Tea. Pitt. Sunday Club."

"Do you belong to that? I thought it was semi-clerical."

"Yes, we are all lay readers."

"I went once," said the Babe. "We ate what is described as a cold collation. Then we all sat round, and somebody made jokes and we all laughed. I made jokes too, but nobody sat round me. There was a delightful, decorous gaiety about the proceedings. I think we sang hymns afterwards, or else we looked at photographs of cathedrals, I forget which. Hymns and photographs are so much alike."

"O Lord, what do you mean?" asked Reggie.

"They are both like Sunday evening, and things which are like the same thing are like one another. At eleven we parted."

"The wicked old Babe doesn't care for simple pleasures," said Ealing. "Oh, he knows a thing or two."

"It's always absurd for a lot of people to meet like that," continued the Babe. "The whole point of dining clubs ought to be to have a lot of members with utterly different tastes. Then you see they can't all talk about their tastes, they can't all sit round and do one thing, and consequently they all talk rot, which is the only rational form of conversation. If there is one thing I detest more than another it is cliques. Individually I love most of the members of the Sunday Club, collectively I cannot even like them. And the same thing applies to the Athenæum."

"Then why do you belong?"

"In order to go to Chapel in a pink and white tie, and also because I love the members individually. I must go. Where's Bill? Come along under my ulster. Good-bye, you people."

V
The Work-club

For men must work.
Kingsley.

Reggie and Ealing were working together. They had formed a work club consisting only of themselves, and it was to meet for the first time this morning. In order to ensure the success of the first meeting they had had a heavy breakfast at a quarter to nine, because, as Reggie said, brain work is more exhausting than anything else, after which they had played a little snob-cricket in the archway between the two halves of Fellows' Buildings, in order to clear the brain, until their names were taken by the porter and entered in the report book. So they adjourned to the bridge for a little to finish their pipes, and about a quarter to eleven sat down one at each side of Reggie's larger table, with a box of cigarettes and a tobacco jar between them, Reggie's alarum clock, which had been induced to go, two copies of Professor Jebb's *Œdipus Tyrannus*, at which they were both working, one small *Liddell & Scott*, and a translation of the play as edited in Mr. Bohn's helpful series of classical authors, in case Professor Jebb proved too free in his translation, "for the difficulties," as Reggie acutely observed, "of rendering Greek both literally and elegantly cannot be over-stated: indeed, it is to be feared that some of our best English scholars sacrifice literal rendering to the latter."

So Ealing threw a sofa cushion at his head, and the alarum clock was knocked over on the floor, and instantly went off. The noise was terrific, and they had to stifle it in a college gown, and put it in the gyp cupboard. Then they began.

For ten minutes or so there was silence, and then Ealing in an abstracted voice asked for the *Liddell & Scott*, and Reggie, not to be behind-hand, underlined one of Professor Jebb's notes with a purple indelible pencil. The point was blunt, and he tried to make it sharper by the aid of a dinner knife. This only resulted in a gradual shortening of the pencil. Also the point became slightly notchier.

Ealing, finding it impossible to go on, while this was being done, had been watching the proceeding at first with deep interest, which passed into a state of wild, unreasonable impatience.

"How clumsy you are," he said at length. "Here, pass it to me. Fancy not being able to sharpen a pencil."

There is, as every one knows, only one individual in the world who can sharpen pencils, and that is oneself. The same remark applies to poking fires. So Reggie replied airily—

"Oh, never mind, old chap. Get on with your work. I can do it beautifully."

But the pencil got rapidly shorter, and in order to prove to his own satisfaction that nobody else in the world could do it, he passed it over to Ealing with the dinner knife. His fingers were purple, and should have been so indelibly, but he hopefully retired into his bedroom to see if it could be washed off.

It was clear at once to Ealing that Reggie's method was altogether at fault, and he rough-hewed the pencil again so as to be able to set to work properly. Then the clock on the mantelpiece, which had been set going, after the alarum became derelict, struck eleven and Reggie returned from his bedroom.

"Of course that clock is fast," said Ealing.

"It's ten minutes slow. Why should you think it was fast?"

"We must have been working longer than I thought. We had breakfast at half-past eight and we began working almost immediately after, didn't we?"

"Yes. We knocked up a bit in the arch, you know."

"Only about ten minutes. I should say we had set to work well before ten."

"Perhaps we did," said Reggie, "but I haven't got through much yet. How's the pencil getting on?"

"Oh, pretty well: but you went the wrong way about it at first!"

"There won't be much left to write with, will there?" asked Reggie, looking at it doubtfully.

"It will last you for weeks with proper care," said Ealing. "I think I never saw so blunt a knife. Why haven't you got a proper knife?"

Reggie got up from the table, and strolled across to the window, and looked out.

"Be quick, old chap," he said. "I can't go on till it's ready. I'm in the middle of underlining something."

He saw an acquaintance below, and called to him.

"The work club's started this morning," he shouted. "We're getting on beautifully."

(Confused sound from below, inaudible to Ealing.)

"Yes, he's just sharpening my pencil. Isn't it kind of him? He says he's getting on with it pretty well."

(Murmur.)

"No, not very far, but I'm in the middle of a chorus, and I'm reading Jebb's notes and marking them."

(Murmur.)

"Oh, hours; ever since about half-past nine or so."

(Murmur.)

"What?"

(Murmur.)

"Yes, Jebb's not literal enough for me. I like to get at the real meaning of— — Oh!"

The sofa cushion flew out of the window and lay on the grass below. When Reggie turned round Ealing was absorbed in his book.

"Where's the pencil?" asked Reggie.

"There isn't any," said Ealing.

"Well, I must go and pick that cushion up. What a lot of time you've made me waste. Also go to Severs's and buy a new pencil. I can't work without."

"This is all the thanks I get," said Ealing bitterly.

"No, I'm awfully obliged to you, but it hasn't done me much good, you know. You see you acted with the best intention, which is always fatal. Where's my cap?"

"I should think you could borrow a pencil," said Ealing.

Reggie considered a moment, with his head on one side.

"I think not. It would be better to get one of my own. Then I shall have one, you see. Come with me?"

The two went down together. As the cushion was lying on the grass, it was necessary to take shots in turn at Reggie's open window, to avoid going upstairs again. This was much more amusing but it took a little longer than the other would have done, and the University clock struck half-past eleven in a slow regretful manner. The successful shot, about which an even sixpence was laid, was made by Ealing, and they crossed King's parade to buy a pencil. As they got to the lodge they were further gratified by the sight of the Babe in the road opposite on a bicycle, which he rode exceedingly badly and with a curious, swoopy, wobbly motion. Mr. Sykes trotted along at a distance of some twenty yards off, with the air of not belonging to anybody, thoroughly ashamed of his master. They called to the Babe, and he being rash enough to try to wave his hand to them, ran straight into the curbstone opposite King's gate, and dismounted hurriedly, stepping into a large puddle. His face was flushed with his exertions, but, as he wrung the water out from the bottom of his trousers, he said genially:

"This is dry work, though it doesn't look it. A small whiskey and soda, Reggie, would not hurt me. No doubt you have such a thing in your room."

"What about Bill Sykes?"

The Babe thought for a moment and mopped his forehead, but in a few seconds a smile of solution lighted his face.

"William shall be chained to the bicycle," he said. "Thus no one will steal the bicycle for fear of William, and William will not venture to run away, as he wouldn't be seen going about the streets with a bicycle in tow for anything. He despises the bicycle. I can hardly make him follow. Come here, darling."

But Mr. Sykes required threats and coaxing. From the first, so the Babe said, he was utterly opposed to the idea of the bicycle, and had, when he thought himself unobserved, been seen to bite it maliciously.

It struck a quarter to twelve.

The Babe was in a peculiarly sociable humour this morning, and after a whiskey and soda, "a cigarette" as he remarked, "would not be amiss," and it was not till he had smoked two, and been told with brutal plainness that he was not wanted in the least, that Reggie discovered that he had forgotten to buy his pencil. This necessitated his and Ealing's making another journey to King's parade, and the Babe, who bore no malice whatsoever at being told to go away, took an arm of each, and insisted in walking across the grass in the hard, convincing light of noonday.

It was now seven minutes past twelve, and opposite the fountain they met the Provost, at the sight of whom the Babe assumed his most affable manner, and they talked together very pleasantly for a minute or two.

"Indeed," as he remarked as they went on their way, "this little meeting should quite take the sting out of the fact that the Porter of your colleges has just retired into his hole in the gate, with the object no doubt, of reporting you both for walking across the grass. And as you have already been reported for playing squash, this will make twice."

Bill Sykes meantime had been the object of much attention on the part of the casual passers-by, and he was sitting there chattering with impotent rage, the centre of a ring of people, in the humiliating position of being chained to a bicycle, which he despised and detested. At the sight of the Babe, however, he forgot for the moment about the bicycle, jumped up, and tried to run towards him. Thus it was not unnatural that the bicycle toppled heavily over onto the top of him. Mr. Sykes was very angry, the bell rang loudly, and one handle of the bicycle was bent.

Mr. Sykes was released, and the Babe who was not expert at mounting, though he said he was the very devil when he got going, hopped slowly down King's Parade for a hundred yards or so with one foot on the step, making ineffectual efforts to get into the saddle. There seemed to be no reason to suppose that he would ever succeed, but about opposite the north end of the Chapel, he accomplished this feat, and after describing two or three graceful but involuntary swoops to the right and left, secured the treadles, and settled comfortably down into one of the tram lines. At this moment the tram came round the corner by St. Mary's, and the bicycle, with its precious burden, seemed doomed to instant annihilation. The Babe, however, got off just in time, and consoled himself by swearing at the driver, and he disappeared among the traffic of Trinity Street still hopping.

"It's like the White Knight riding," said Ealing. "Look sharp, Reggie, with that beastly pencil. It's struck a quarter past."

Between one thing and another, it was creditable that they were ready to begin work again at half-past twelve. Reggie finished underlining his note, the point of which he could not quite understand, and so put a query in the margin, and Ealing went back to the word he was looking out in *Liddell &* *Scott*, an hour and a quarter before.

Ten minutes later Reggie observed that the Babe had forgotten his cover-coat, which was lying on a chair, and they debated with some heat whether it had better be taken to him at once. Eventually they tossed up, as to who should do it; Ealing lost the toss, and they both jumped up with alacrity.

"It's a beastly nuisance when one has just settled down to work again," he said.

"I won," remarked Reggie, "and I am going. By Jove, there's that Varsity clock striking a quarter to one. Here, let's both go. It's no use working for a quarter of an hour. One can't do anything in a quarter of an hour, and I must lunch at one, as I'm playing footer."

"All right. Of course we work after tea for two hours more as we settled. That will make five, and one more after Hall."

"And six hours steady work a day," said Reggie cheerfully, "is as much as is good for any man. I begin not to attend after I have worked, really worked, you know, for six hours."

VI
The Babe's Picnic

Row, brothers, row,
The stream runs slow,
We don't know how to row
And the oars stick so.
Light-blue Lyrics.

The Babe was no waterman, and he never pretended to be, but this did not prevent his getting up a quiet picnic on the upper river one delightful afternoon towards the end of May. There were only to be four of them, not counting Mr. Sykes—though it was impossible not to count Mr. Sykes, the others being Reggie, Ealing, and Jack Marsden.

Marsden, who had once, when a Freshman, been coached on the river, by an angry man in shorts, and had been abandoned as hopeless after his first trial, was naturally supposed by the Babe to be an accomplished oarsman, and to have probed to its depths the nature of boats and oars and stretchers, so he was deputed to find a boat which held four people, several hampers, and a dog, and

TRINITY BRIDGE, FROM THE BACKS.

which was warranted not to shy or bolt, and to be quiet with children. It was understood that the Babe was not going to row or steer, his office being merely to provide food for them all, and if possible to prevent Mr. Sykes from leaping overboard when they passed the bathing-sheds, and biting indiscriminately at the bathers, whom for some reason of his own he regarded with peculiar but perfectly ineradicable disfavour. The Babe had taken him up the river only the week before, but opposite the town sheds Sykes had been unable to restrain himself, had jumped off the boat into the water and chased to land a bland and timid shopkeeper, to whom the Babe owed money, so it looked as if it was a put-up job; the man had regained the steps of the bathing-shed only just in time to save himself from being pinned in the calf of the leg.

The Babe and Jack were to start from the raft by Trinity at three, and pick up Reggie and Ealing opposite King's. They were then to row up to Byron's Pool (so-called because there is no reason to suppose that Byron was not extremely fond of it,) bathe and have tea, and afterwards go a mile or so farther, and have dinner. The Babe who just now was gated at ten, confidently hoped to be home at or before that hour, on the sole ground that Napoleon had once said there was no such word as impossible.

They paddled quietly up to the Mill just above the town, and here it was necessary to haul the boat over the bank separating the upper river from the lower. The Babe who was beautifully dressed in white flannels, yellow boots, and a straw hat with a new riband, courteously declined giving the smallest assistance to the others, but watched the operation with interest and apparent approval, in consequence of which he was advised by Reggie, who had got hot and rather dirty with his exertions, to drop that infernally patronising attitude. Here too Mr. Sykes first sniffed the prey, for he had caught sight of the bathers at the town sheds across the fields, and was trotting quietly off in their direction, secretly licking his lips, but outwardly pretending that he was merely going for a little airy walk on his own account. The Babe had to run after him and haul him back, for he affected to hear neither whistling nor shouting, and on his return he kept smelling suspiciously at the legs of casual passers-by as if he rather suspected that they were going to bathe too.

Though the lower river is one of the foulest streams on the face of the earth, the upper river is one of the fairest. It wanders up between fresh green fields, bordered by tall yellow flags, loosestrife, and creamy meadow-sweet, all unconscious of the fate that awaits it from vile man below. Pollarded willows lean over the bank and listen to the wind, and here and there a company of white poplars, the most distinguished of trees, come trooping down to the water's edge. The stream itself carpeted with waving weeds strolls along clear and green from the reflection of the trees, troops of bleak poise and dart in the shallows, or shelter in the subaqueous forests, and the Babe said he saw a trout, a statement to which no importance whatever need be attached. Looking back across a mile of fields you see the pinnacles of King's rise grey and grave into the sky; and in front, Granchester, with its old-fashioned garden-cradled houses, presided over by a church tower on the top of which, as a surveyor once remarked, there is a plus sign which is useful as a fixed point, nestles in a green windless hollow.

But Bill, like Gallio, cared for none of those things. He knew perfectly well that they were going to pass the town bathing-place very shortly, and after half a mile or so more of uninteresting river, the University bathing-place. The Babe had taken him up here once when he had bathed himself, and though Mr. Sykes realised that he must not bite his master, whatever foolish and ungentlemanly thing he chose to do, he was very cold and reserved to him afterwards. But he meant to behave exactly as he pleased at the town bathing-place, and a hundred yards before they got there, he was standing in the bow of the boat, uttering short malignant growls. The Babe, however, pulled him back by the tail, and muffled him up in four towels, and Mr. Sykes rolled about the bottom of the boat, and from within the towels came sounds of deep dissatisfaction just as if there were a discontented bull-pup in the middle of them.

Beyond the town bathing-place stands a detached garden, with bright flower-beds cut out in a lawn of short green turf. Here the Babe conceived a violent desire to land and have tea, which he was not permitted to do; and above that runs a stretch of river, very properly known as Paradise, seeing which the Babe had a fit of rusticity and said he would go no farther, but live evermore under the trees with Mr. Sykes, and grow a honey-coloured beard. He would encamp under the open sky, and on fine afternoons would be seen sitting on the river bank dabbling his feet in the water, and playing on a rustic pipe made of reeds. He would keep a hen and a cow and a bed of strawberries, and it should be always a summer afternoon. Indeed, had not a water-rat been seen at the moment, which compelled him to throw Mr. Sykes overboard to see whether he could catch it,—which he could not—there is no knowing what developments this rustic phase would have undergone. So they went slowly on, making a small detour up to the Granchester Mill, where the water came hurrying out cool and foamy, and where the Babe asked an elderly man, who was fishing intently on the bank, whether he had had any bites, which seemed to infuriate him strangely, for he was fishing with a fly; drifted down again under a big chestnut tree, all covered with pyramids of white blossoms, and turned up the left arm of the river. The water was shallower here, and now and then gravelly shoals appeared above the surface. They frequently ran aground, and made no less than three futile attempts to get round a sharp corner, where the stream running swiftly took the nose of the boat into the bank, and the Babe swore gently at them all, and told them to mark the finish, and get their hands away.

A long lane of quiet shallow water leads to the tail of the pool, and here the river spreads out into a broad deep basin. Grey sluice gates, flanked with red brick form the head of it, and on one side stretches out a green meadow, on the other there rises out of an undergrowth of hazel and hemlock, a copse of tall trees, where the nightingales always omit to sing. They ran the boat in at the edge of the copse, and Reggie lighted the spirit lamp to boil the kettle for tea, while the Babe tied up Mr. Sykes, lest he should forget himself at the sight of four bathers.

Among sensuous pleasures, bathing on a hot day stands alone, and Byron's Pool is in the first flight of bathing places. There are some who prefer Romney Weir, and say that bathing is nought unless you plunge into a soda water of bubbles; some think that the essence of bathing is a mere pickling of the human form in brine, and are not happy except in the sea; to others the *joie de baigner* consists of flashing through the air much as M. Doré has pictured Satan falling down from Heaven. But in Byron's Pool the reflective, or what we may call the garden bather is well off. He has clean water deep to the edge, a grassy slope shadowed by trees to dry on, and a boat to take a header from. Even Mr. Stevenson, a precisian in these matters, would allow "that the imagination takes a share in such a cleansing." And by the time they were dressed, the kettle was boiling, and Fortune smiled on them.

The Babe refused, however, to stir before he had drunk four cups of tea, and in consequence the kettle had to be boiled again.

"Besides," said he, "Mr. Sykes hasn't had his second cup."

It was generally felt that this was more important than the Babe's fourth cup, and Reggie filled the kettle.

"The Babe's pensive," he said, "What is it, Babe?"

"I don't know. Sometimes I get pensive on fine days or on wet evenings, but it doesn't usually last long. I think I want to fall in love."

"Well it's May week next week."

"One is always supposed to fall in love with each other's sisters in May week," remarked the Babe with a fine disregard of grammar. "But the sisters either die of consumption or else the Dean snaps them up, and so it doesn't come off. Besides one so seldom does what one is supposed to do."

"Not often. Byron was supposed to bathe here for instance, and you are supposed to be in by ten to-night, Babe."

"Napoleon said—" began the Babe.

"Dry up. Why did they gate you?"

"For repeated warnings, I believe. I never asked them to warn me. They go and warn me," said the Babe, getting a little shrill, "and then they go and gate me for it. I have been allowed no voice whatever in the matter."

"What did they warn you about?"

"Oh, it was Bill and the bicycle between them, and the time, and the place. Life is a sad business, and mine is a hard lot."

"You are a bad lot," suggested Jack.

"Jack, for God's sake don't be funny," said Ealing.

"I thought the Babe wanted a little cheering up. I know he likes being called a bad lot. He isn't really."

"It is quite true," said the Babe in a hollow voice. "I have tried to go to the devil, and I can't. It is the most tedious process. Virtue and simplicity are stamped on my face and my nature. I am like Queen Elizabeth. I was really cut out to be a milkmaid. I don't want to get drunk, or to cultivate the lower female. The more wine I drink, the sleepier I get; I have to pinch myself to keep awake, and I should be sleeping like a dead pig long before I got the least intoxicated. Even then if you woke me up I could say the most difficult words like Ranjitsinghi without the least incoherence. And as for the lower female—well, I had to wait at the station the other day for half an hour, so I thought it was a good opportunity to talk to the barmaid at the refreshment room. So I ordered a whiskey and soda and called her 'Miss.' I did indeed."

"What a wicked Babe."

"I did call her Miss. 'Miss,' I tell you," shouted the Babe. "Then I said it was a beautiful day, and she said 'Yes, dear.' She called me 'dear,' and I submitted. I didn't throw the whiskey and soda at her, I didn't call for help or give her in charge. I determined to go through with it. She was a mass of well-matured charms, and she breathed heavily through her nose. Round her neck she had a massive silver locket on with 'Pizgah,' or 'Kibroth Hataavah,' or 'Jehovah Nisi' upon it."

"Decree Nisi," suggested Ealing.

"She looked affectionately at me," continued the Babe, "and a cold shudder ran through me. She asked me if I would treat her to a glass of port, *port*, at a quarter-past four in the afternoon. I said, 'By all means,' and she pulled a sort of lever, the kind of thing you put a train into a siding with, and out came port, which she drank. Then she said smilingly, "Aven't seen you for a long time,' which was quite true, as I'd never set foot in the place before, and she won't see me again for an equally long time. I waited there ten minutes, ten whole ghastly minutes, and the words froze on my tongue, and the thoughts in my brain. For the life of me I could not think of another thing to say. She continued to smile at me all the time. She smiled for ten minutes without stopping. And so we parted. The kettle is boiling, Reggie."

The Babe mixed Mr. Sykes's second cup for him and drank his fourth.

"It is no use," he said. "I am irredeemably silly, and I have no other characteristic whatever. My golden youth is slipping from me in the meantime."

Reggie shouted.

"The Babe thinks he is growing old. We don't agree with him. Of course he is old in everything else, but not in years. Babe, if you're ready we'll go on. We've got to haul the boat over here."

The Babe jumped up with sudden alacrity.

"All right. Mr. Sykes and I will get out. We shall only be in the way. Come on, Bill."

"No, Babe," said Jack, "you shirked before. You shall at least carry the hampers."

"I shall do nothing of the kind," said the Babe with dignity, and on this point he was quite polite but perfectly firm.

They rowed a mile or so farther up, and the Babe selected a suitable place for dinner, at the edge of a hayfield and under a willow tree, and a smile of kind indulgence towards the world in general began to overscore his fruitless regrets of the afternoon. It was after eight when they began dinner, and the Babe's commissariat was plentiful and elaborate. The only dish that failed to give satisfaction was the toasted cheese with which he insisted they should finish dinner. It was made in the tea kettle, and when melted, poured out through the spout on to biscuits. Mr. Sykes and the Babe alone attempted to eat it, and Mr. Sykes who ate less than the Babe was excessively unwell shortly afterwards.

"But for that," said the Babe, drinking Chartreuse out of a tea-cup, "I blame the lobster."

The moon, as big as a bandbox, was just rising clear of the trees, and the Babe produced cigars.

"For mine," he said, "is one of those rare, generous natures that does unto others what it would not do unto itself. It all comes in the catechism. I will thank any one for a simple paper cigarette."

"Speech," said Ealing. "As Stewart."

The Babe bowed, and began, drawling out his words in a low, slow, musical voice.

"Mr. Sykes and gentlemen," he said, "the May week is upon us, and we, like the *Cambridge Review*, are at the end of another year of University life and thought. Some of us—most of us in fact, have experienced for two years the widening influence and varied duties which are inseparable from the minds of any of those who embark upon the harvest of University curriculum with any earnestness of purpose, or seriousness of aim. I think, in fact, I am right in believing that my friend Mr. Reginald Bristow alone—to continue a few of my less mixed metaphors—has put out only a year's space upon the sea of those special features, which mark the career and are the hinge of the prospects of those miners after perfectly useless knowledge who seek to increase their general ignorance among the purlieus of Alma Mater. Some of us have failed in attaining the objects of our various ambitions, and I am happy to say that none of us have really tried to do so. We have none of us gone to the devil, and he with characteristic exclusiveness has kept aloof from us all. [Cheers] We none of us play cricket for the University, though I once knew a man who got his extra square at chess; he was a dear boy, but he is dead now, and there is not the slightest fear that anything will prevent us from being unable to fail in obtaining a very respectable place in our Triposes. Yes, the May week, which occurs in June and lasts a fortnight, spoken of, I may say sung of in the pages of the *Junior Dean* and *The Fellow of Trinity*, is upon us. Personally I detest the May week and I am subscribing to the Grace testimonial fund simply and solely because I abhor the boat procession, but before long our stately chapels and storied urns [cheers] will echo to the sound of girlish laughter and maternal feet. Gentlemen, I thank you from the bottom of my heart for the very sincere way in which this toast has been received, and am happy to declare that the Institution is now open, and the meeting adjourned *sine die*."

· · · · · ·

Going home, the Babe had to stand in the bows to look out for snags and shoals. He carried a lantern in his hand by the light of which he scrutinised with agonised intentness the dark surface of the water. Just above Byron's Pool the boat ran into a sunken tree trunk and the Babe and his lantern plunged heavily into the water. So he dressed himself in the tablecloth, and his appearance was inimitable. He did not stop in Cambridge for the May week.

VII
The Babe's "Sapping"

Lo, when an oyster, succulent and tender,
Leagued with lemon, courted by cayenne,
Makes its inevitable sweet surrender,
Delicately dies, it knows not why or when,—

"Could aught atone?" pathetically asked he,
He whom ye wot, to find that unaware
Oysters would be indubitably nasty,
Natives or not, because July is here?
St. Swithin.

The Babe spent June and the first half of July in London. He painted his bicycle white with Mr. Aspinall's best enamel, and presented a very elegant appearance on it every morning in Battersea Park. The elections were on, and his father, who represented the Conservative interests of a manufacturing town in the North of England, was absent from London, in the hopes of representing them again. But party questions did not interest his son, and the Babe, reflecting that whether the Liberals or Conservatives governed the country, Battersea Park would still be open to him and his bicycle, pursued his calm course on a moderately evenly-balanced wheel.

So the Babe had a commodious house in Prince's Gate at his disposal. For he was the only child, and his mother, who was a keener politician even than his father, accompanied the latter on his political errands. It occurred to him that he might turn an honest penny by letting the whole of the first floor for a week or two after the manner of Mr. Somerset, when he found himself in possession of the Superfluous Mansion, but after some consideration, he dismissed this as an unworthy and inconvenient economy, and telegraphed to Reggie to leave Cambridge and the May week to take care of themselves and join him. Reggie had kept his term, so he obeyed, taking with him several classical books, for the Babe, so he said in his telegram, meant to "sap."

The Babe's "sapping" was conducted on highly original principles. He got up at eight, "in order," he said, "to get a long morning," had a cup of tea, and then took his bicycle with him in his mother's victoria to Battersea Park, where he rode till ten, and then had breakfast. He got back to Prince's Gate about eleven in the victoria which waited for him at the Park, had a bath and dressed, and usually went off to Lord's where he watched cricket till lunch time from the top of the pavilion, and if the match was interesting stopped on till about five. He then went to the Bath Club where he bathed and had tea, returning home in time to dress for dinner, which he usually took at a friend's house. The evening was spent at a theatre or a music hall, and he finished up if possible at a dance. If he had no dance to go to, he read the evening paper at a club, and went to bed.

"In fact," as he explained to Reggie, who arrived one evening about seven, "we shall lead a simple and strenuous life even in the midst of this modern Babylon. The bicycle and the Bath Club will minister to the needs of the body, and our minds will minister to each other. We take our dinner to-night at home, and after dinner it would be rash not to see Miss Cecilia Loftus. She can dance like fun. I hope you have brought some books, for otherwise you will have nothing to do when I am working. It's time to dress. I see my father made four speeches yesterday. His energy is perfectly amazing. We will send for the evening paper, for there are things of overwhelming interest in it, I am told, apart from politics."

The programme at the "Pavilion" waned in interest after the performance of Miss Cecilia Loftus, and about eleven the Babe proposed an adjournment. It was a warm clear night, and they started back, walking along Piccadilly instead of taking a hansom. The streets were full, and characteristically "London," in other words they were crowded with all sorts and conditions of men and women, who eyed one another with suspicious reserve. In Paris the birds of night look at each other with friendly interest, in London with mistrust and enmity.

The Babe was in an expansive mood, and like Byron, he bitterly lamented his own loneliness in the crowd.

"Here am I," he said, "a young man of pleasing manner, and amiable disposition, and I feel like a solitary wayfarer in the desert of Sahara. When the four men in the *New Arabian Nights* left Prince Florizel's smoking divan, and plunged into the roaring streets, they were engulfed by strange adventures before they had gone a hundred yards. The Lady of the Superfluous Mansion annexed one, the Fair Cuban another, the man with the chin beard a third. What could be more delightful? And yet I might walk the streets till the crack of doom, and the archangels would have to send me home at the last, still adventureless."

"Poor Babe," said Reggie, "but perhaps every one else is in the same plight; perhaps they are all longing for you to speak to them."

"I don't think so," said the Babe, "they seem to me supremely indifferent as to whether I speak to them or not. What are we to do, Reggie? The night is yet young, but we are growing old. I think a little supper, four or five dozen native lobsters, as Mrs. Nickleby suggested, would not hurt us. I hear that there is a most commodious restaurant at the Savoy Hotel. It would be well to be certain on that point. We are walking in the wrong direction but we will do so no longer. Let us take a hansom. Nothing will happen to us. But we will give this wicked world one more chance. We will walk back across Leicester Square. It is supposed to be the fountain-head of all adventures, and the home of all adventurers. We will loiter there a few moments."

"What sort of adventures do you want, Babe?" asked Reggie.

"Why that's exactly what I couldn't tell you," said the Babe, "the point of an adventure is that it is absolutely unexpected. If I could tell you what I wanted, it would cease to be unexpected, and therefore cease to be an adventure. If you know what you are going to do, it is no adventure. But it's no use: unexpected things never happen. We will take a cab and eat oysters. Perhaps the oysters will be stale, and if so, it will be a kind of adventure, for they are invariably fresh at the Savoy."

The Babe selected a table in the balcony opening out of the restaurant; below they could see the long gaslit line of embankment curving gently towards Westminster, and the river flowing turbidly out with the ebbing tide. In the middle distance the bridge of Charing Cross with one great electric lamp high in the air, crossed to the Surrey side, and every now and then a train shrieked across under the glass arch of the station. In the street below there jingled by, from time to time, a hansom, noiseless except for the bell, and the sharp-cut ring of the horse's hoofs. A party of shrill-voiced Americans took a table near them, and discussed the relative merits of English and American cars, with passionate partisanship. There were of course no oysters to be had, as it was June, and native devilled kidneys had to take their place. Tired-looking waiters flitted noiselessly about, and the Babe's face caught from the kidneys a livelier animation.

"To-morrow," he said, "we will go even unto the Oval, and watch the gentlemen and players. It is strange that to play cricket is the most doleful of human pursuits, and to watch it one of the most delightful. When I grow up I shall keep twenty-two men who shall play cricket before me, as Salome danced before Herod. They shall play a perpetual match, which shall never come to a world without end. Amen. Have some more kidneys, Reggie? A few of our small kidneys would not hurt you. Waiter, bring some more kidneys. Kidneys are not attractive to the eye, but the proof of them is in the eating. I eat them because they are so comfortable, as the Psalmist says. By the way, has Sir John Lubbock put the eating of kidneys among his *Pleasures of Life*? I shall write a book called *The Sorrows of Death* as a companion volume."

"Do; and have it set to music by Mendelssohn."

"Mendelssohn is dead, and the kidneys are dead," said the profane Babe. "Hullo there's Stewart. He looks like a man out of the *Yellow Book* by Aubrey Beardsley. I wish I could look as if Aubrey Beardsley had drawn me; shall I ask him to supper, Reggie? I wonder what he's doing at the Savoy?"

But Mr. Stewart had got a Cabinet Minister in hand just for the present, and it was half an hour or so before he joined them; even then it took him ten minutes to get through the amiability of Cabinet Ministers, before descending to more sublunary topics. But when he descended, as the Babe said afterwards, he came down with a run, and talked about music-halls and other things.

He was most sympathetic with the Babe's misfortune in being unable to stop up for May week, and inveighed against the government and management of the University generally.

"It is incredible to me," he said, "perfectly incredible that so much pedantry and narrowness can be compressed into so small a place. There is not a single one of my colleagues whom I could call a man of the world. I was saying just now to my dear friend Abbotsbury who has been very strongly urging me to stand for Cambridge in Parliament, that I am really quite unfit, perfectly unfit to represent the University. I know nothing whatever about my colleagues, and I disapprove of all I know of them. Take your own case. You are of years of discretion, my dear Babe, and if you choose to dress in a tablecloth, no one has any right to prevent you. They wouldn't have any right to stop you if you chose to dress in two—less right in fact. I'm sure you looked charming in a tablecloth. Why should the Dean of your college exercise jurisdiction over your dress? He is no Prince Regent. For he dresses himself in a cake hat and a tail coat, which is perhaps the least becoming style of dress which can be conceived. Yet he isn't sent down for it. Why should he be allowed to make the Great Court of Trinity hideous, and you be sent down for—for making it beautiful?"

"The Babe did a skirt dance down Malcolm Street," remarked Reggie, "and it was a windy night."

"Well, the Babe isn't to blame if it is a windy night," said Mr. Stewart. "They had probably been praying for wind in St. Mary's, though the only time in my life that I attended a University sermon there was plenty of wind. The sermon was preached by a black missionary, who I think said he came from Iceland, which I don't believe. He literally swept us away in a hurricane of inconsequent appeal. Really to assume that the Babe is responsible for the wind, is almost profanity. What a delicious night! It quite makes me think of the feasts of Tiberius at Capri. The air is as soft as the air of Naples and all the waiters here, as at Capri, are made in Germany. Germany itself, I believe, is getting gradually depopulated, and I 'm sure I don't wonder. Yes, I am staying here for a day or two. There is an expensive simplicity about the Savoy, which almost lets me forget for the time the pompous cheapness both literal and literary of University towns. Oxford is no better. Dons think about croquet and Triposes at Cambridge, and about Moderations and lawn tennis at Oxford. It is six of one and five and a half of the other. And the *cuisine* of the college kitchens is enough to make Savarin turn in his grave. You order melted butter, and they bring forth milk in a crockery dish."

"I thought you were devoted to Cambridge," said Reggie. "I'm sure I've heard you say so."

"Dear Reggie, let me ask you never to remember anything I say. But it is true that I am devoted to what I consider to be the *raison d'être* of Cambridge, that is the undergraduates, with their fresh bright lives, and their *insouciance,* their costumes of tablecloths and their frank contempt for the class to which I have the misfortune to belong. That is why I always go up in the Long, dons for the time are in eclipse: it is like a whole holiday. I am going there next week, to stop for a month or so. I hope you are both coming."

"Yes," said the Babe, "we are both going up to work. I am to go in for a tripos in history instead of a pass. I had a short and painful interview with my father about it. Why are fathers so curt? Do you suppose I shall get through?"

"A tripos," remarked Mr. Stewart, "is a form of self-mutilation. To go in for a tripos, if you are not by nature tripical, if I may coin a word, and I may tell you that it is to your credit that you are not, my dear Babe, implies a sacrifice of other branches of your nature. Why cannot fathers be content to let their sons be, and not do? No one yet has ever been able to tell me of any good thing that comes out of triposes, except that it keeps the Examiners to their rooms for three weeks afterwards. But they come out like pigmies refreshed with small beer, and talk about quadratic calculus and deliberative genitives with redoubled vigour. The test which triposes apply discovers whether the candidates are possessed of a little knowledge, and so are dangerous things. If they helped them to realise the beauty of ancient Athens, or the picturesqueness of the French Revolution, it would be a different matter and I, as I understood Longridge to do the other day at a College meeting, should advocate having a tripos once a week and twice on Sundays. But all they do is to instil into the minds of the undergraduates a confused and it may be an incorrect idea, that all Athenians were as great a bore as Thucydides and spoke as bad Greek, and that there is a grave doubt whether, after all, Marie Antoinette died by the guillotine, and was not carried off by an attack of acute old age at the age of eighty-seven. Even if it was so, and it is far from certain, why tell any one about it? History rightly considered is a great and wonderful romance, and the methods employed at places of education is to render sterile all the germs of romance it contains, and condense the residue of facts into the smallest possible compass, and Mr. Stanley Weyman then proceeds to write reliable blue books about them, which his publisher libellously advertises as "New Novels," though they are neither new nor novel. One of my colleagues just before the tripos, circulated among his pupils a half-sheet of paper, not very closely printed. But that infernal half-sheet contained all the procedure of the Athenian law courts, and if learned by heart, quite unintelligently, as he recommended, would insure full marks on any question that might be set on the subject. I had the misfortune to be with him when one of his pupils returned from the examination, and he literally danced for joy all over the Combination Room, though he is a stout man, when he saw that three questions out of nine could be completely answered from his repulsive little half-sheet. And the tripos in the face of these revolting details, is called a test of a man's ability, and goes a long way to win him a Fellowship. You, my dear Babe, are a man of far more liberal education than that lamentable colleague of mine, though, I may say, in answer to your question, that I would only take very long odds if I had to bet on your chance of getting through."

"I got through my last May's," remarked the Babe in self-defence.

"Yes, but without incriminating myself, my dear boy, I must remind you that I looked over at least three of your papers, and the marks I gave you were more for your capability of acquiring romantic and delightful knowledge, and for a certain power of giving plausible and voluminous answers to questions of which it was obvious you knew nothing whatever, than the actual knowledge your papers displayed. However if you come down to little half-sheets of useless and absurd facts, no doubt you will be able to get through, and it is upon that, that I would take only very long odds. From what I know of you, I do not think you will come down to that. I am delighted to hear you are coming up in the Long, and we will read some charming French memoirs together. They are much more amusing, and much more picturesque than Zola's tedious pictures of the Second Empire. Reggie, you are classical, are you not? Read, mark, and learn the *Phædrus*, and the *Symposium*. The former you should read on the upper river under a plane tree if possible, the latter after dining wisely and well in your rooms, and you will know more of the essential Greek than all Mackintyre's horrid little half-sheets could ever teach you."

"Then do you think the tripos is perfectly useless and valueless?" asked the Babe.

"Absolutely so: and what makes it more ridiculous is that it is not even ornamental. Most useless things have some beauty or charm about them. The tripos alone, as far as I know, has none. I have only done one thing in my life of which I am thoroughly ashamed, and that is that I took a first in my tripos. Mackintyre of course did the same. It is the thing in his life—he was Senior Classic I think—of which he is most proud. However, to do him justice, I believe that of late years what is called the Philatelic Society has usurped most of his leisure time. No, it has nothing to do with telepathy; it means loving things that are a long way off and is specialised to apply to collections of postage stamps. To me the word denotes 'Distance lends enchantment to the view.'"

The Babe was continuing to eat strawberries with a pensive air while Mr. Stewart spoke, and having finished the dish he looked round plaintively, and Reggie caught his eye.

"You mustn't eat any more, Babe," he said, "it's after twelve, and we're going out at eight to-morrow, and we have to get back to Prince's Gate."

The Babe sighed.

"Mr. Sykes will be waiting up for us," he said; "I suppose we ought to go. He will lose his beauty-sleep."

VIII
A Game of Croquet

So the Babe took Reggie's queen, which for the last eight moves had led a dog's life, and Reggie lost his temper and upset the board intentionally. Mr. Sykes who was lying on the hearth-rug, pretended that the black king was a rat, though of course he knew it was not, and proceeded to worry it.

In other words it was just after lunch on Monday the 7th of August. They had lunched in Hall, and a Fellow of the college, who rejoiced in the name of Gingham had asked them to play croquet afterwards in the King's garden at half-past two. There was no cricket going on, and it was too hot to play tennis, so they very kindly consented.

The black king was rescued, and the Babe tucked Mr. Sykes under his arm and shut him into Reggie's gyp closet, as the sight of a croquet ball always inspired him with a wild, chattering rage, and they strolled out onto the bridge to wait for Gingham, who appeared before long accompanied by a colleague from another college, of mean appearance, who proved also to be of uncertain temper.

The limes down to the back gate were in full flower and resonant with bees, and Mr. Gingham made a very felicitous quotation from the fourth Georgic with gay facility. Beyond, the road along the Backs lay cool and white beneath the enormous elms, and the Babe asserted that he heard a nightingale, which Mr. Gingham's friend said was quite impossible, since it was the end of the first week in August. But the Babe remarked with a fatuous smile, that he had been Senior Ornithologist, and might be supposed to know. Upon which Mr. Gingham's friend said there was no such thing as an Ornithological tripos, and the Babe replied: "That's a Loring," and refused to explain further.

Behind the railings the garden lay deliciously fresh and green. Long, level plains of grass were spread about between the flower-beds, and the whole place had an air of academic and cultivated repose. On one of these stretches of lawn a game of tennis was in progress; the performance was not of a very high class, but the players seemed to be enjoying themselves.

Each game opened with a regularity which to the ordinary mind would appear monotonous in incessant repetition. The first service delivered by all the players was a swift, splendid fault served low into the net, and this was invariably followed by a slow underhand service, always perfectly faultless, but probably easy of execution. Then, however, a pleasing diversity varied the progress of the rest. About sixty per cent. of these services were returned, in which case the partner of the server, who stood close up to the net, hit them cruelly out of court and called the score in an angry, rasping voice, as if it had been contradicted. The other forty per cent. came to an untimely end in the meshes of the net. But the interest of the game to the Babe, who lagged behind to watch it for a few minutes, was, that whereas most people who play lawn-tennis indifferently are exactly like everybody else, these four players seemed to him to be like nobody else. One of them was so glaringly obscure that you would scarcely have known he was there, if you had not seen him returning the balls; the second was more neglected by nature than one would have thought a living man could be, and had the sleeves of his shirt buttoned round his wrists; the third had a face which resembled only the face of an emaciated man seen in the bowl of a spoon, and the features of the fourth were obscured by a hat which resembled a beehive in shape, and a frieze coat in texture, but on the doctrine of probabilities, it seemed likely that, did we know all, he would have proved to be as remarkable as his fellow sportsmen. He whisked about with astonishing rapidity, though he was hardly ever in his right place, and a handkerchief which dangled out of his trousers pocket reminded the observer of a white, badly-trimmed tail.

The Babe's curiosity to see his face grew unbearable, but, like the Quangle-Wangle, his face was not to be seen. Once the Babe thought he caught sight of a small, round, open mouth, but he could not be sure.

The name of Mr. Gingham's colleague was Jones, and he and Gingham played the Babe and Reggie. Jones began, but failed at the second hoop, and the Babe having passed it, croquetted him cheerfully away into a fine big bush about one hundred yards distant. He said to Jones, in his genial way: "An enemy hath done this," but got no reply. He then tried to get into position for the third hoop, and it is doubtful whether in all the annals of croquet, there was ever made so vilely futile a stroke. Gingham followed, and as it was hopeless to mobilise with a ball a hundred yards off, took a shot at the Babe's ball, got through the third hoop, and secured position for the cage. Reggie mobilised with the Babe, and then there was a pause, broken by a confused but angry murmur from inside a beautiful laurestinus now in full flower. It is almost needless to explain that Jones could not find his ball. When he did discover it, he took it out and made an extraordinarily good attempt to get into position for the second hoop, but just hit the wire, and lay in a bee-line with the opening. He lit a cigarette and tried to kick the match with which he had lit it.

Then it was that Satan entered into the Babe's soul, and from this point an analysis of Jones's strokes is worth recording.

(I.)   Secured position for the second hoop.

(II.)   Tried to regain position for the second hoop.

(III.)   Wired for the second hoop.

(IV.)   A curious stroke in which the cage was torn up and twisted as if by some convulsion of Nature, and had to be replaced in position and straightened.

(V.)   Hit the Babe's ball, but played out of turn. Ball replaced, and stroke played again. No result, but left near the further stump.

(VI.)   Failed to secure position for the second hoop.

(VII.)   Secured position for the second hoop.

(VIII.)   A cross-country hit from below the willow-tree into the same beautiful laurestinus.

(IX.)   Captured the Babe's ball, and sent it to the feet of the man with the beehive hat.

(X.)
(XI.)   } Returned by stages to the second hoop.

(XII.)   Sent the Babe through the cage by accident.

(XIII.)   Secured position for the second hoop.

At this point Mr. Jones gave vent to a most regrettable remark about the Babe, and his nose swelled a little. Such a result was excusable, for the Babe's diabolical ingenuity in attacking him had only been equalled by his diabolical luck. Twice,—for the ground was not well-rolled—had his ball come skipping and hopping along, and had pounced upon his adversary's like a playful kitten, and twice he had cannoned violently off a hoop onto it. But about this point his luck had shown signs of failing, and he sheltered himself for a few strokes near his partner, who together with Gingham had been plodding slowly and steadily round the hoops. Altogether the game had been like "Air with Variations," the Babe and Mr. Jones taking brilliant firework excursions across the theme. But for a little while it seemed as if the cup of the Babe's iniquities was full, and for ten minutes he kept falling into the hand of his adversaries with the most surprising persistence. But the end was not yet.

Half an hour later the position was as follows:

Reggie and Gingham were rovers, the Babe had not been through the cage coming back, but Jones had only the two last hoops to pass, and it was Jones's turn. The Babe was getting a little excited, and the lust for vengeance was on Jones. He had even gone so far as to advise the Babe what to do on one occasion, and the Babe had answered him shortly in a high, tremulous voice.

The Babe's ball was in position for the cage, and theoretically Jones was wired to him. But his ball, violently and maliciously struck, curled in a complicated manner off the cage wires and hit the Babe's.

"That's a beastly fluke," said that gentleman in an excited contralto.

Jones could afford to be generous.

"It did turn it off a little," he said pacifically, "but I think it would have hit it anyhow."

"Then you think wrong," said the Babe outwardly calm.

The laurestinus quivered.

Jones became a rover, and mobilised with his partner, but not very close.

The Babe failed to mobilise with Reggie.

Gingham shot at his partner and missed.

Reggie mobilised successfully with the Babe.

Quem deus vult perdere, prius dementat. Jones ought to have separated them but having hit his partner, he tried to put him out, failed, but left himself and his partner both close to the stump.

The Babe smiled, and there was a tea-party of four. He smiled again a little unkindly. He put Gingham out, and he hit Jones's ball. A moment afterwards a frenzied croquet ball bounded into the net of the tennis-players, and caused the spoon-faced man, for the first time that afternoon, to serve two consecutive faults. Then the Babe went back to his hoop. Gingham was of a peaceful disposition but rather timid. He had, however, caught a glimpse of Jones's face as he walked off to the lawn-tennis court, and it might reasonably, he said afterwards, have frightened a bolder man than he. So he turned to the Babe.

"You know it's only a game," he said, and the Babe replied still rather shrilly:

"Then watch me play it."

Reggie and the Babe between them could easily keep Mr. Jones's ball safely off the ground, and the Babe plodded on till he too was a rover, and Reggie and he went out in the next two turns.

"A very pleasant game," said he smiling.

Jones was ill-advised enough to murmur:

"Insolent young ass."

The Babe heard and his face turned pink, but his smile suffered no diminution.

"A very pleasant game," he repeated, "but only a game."

IX
Tea at the Pitt

Dark house by which once more I stand
Here in the long unlovely street.—Tennyson.

The Babe was leaning out of the window of the rooms he had moved into for the Long, which looked onto the Great Court of Trinity, and in his hands was a simple sheet of foolscap paper rolled up big at one end and small at the other. He applied his mouth intermittently to the small end of this really elementary contrivance, and, in his hands, like the sonnet in the hand of Milton, "the thing became a trumpet." Unlike Milton, however, he was in no way liable to censure for not using it often enough.

He had been working for nearly two hours that morning, and it was only just half-past eleven. He had got up at eight, breakfasted, and had really been at it ever since. As a rule, criticisms on himself did not make the least impression on him, but somehow or other Mr. Stewart's unwillingness to take any but the longest odds on the subject of his getting through the tripos had struck root and grown up rankling in his mind. He knew quite well that he had as much ability as many undergraduates who tackle that examination successfully, and he believed that if he chose he could acquire a sufficient portion of their industry. Hence the early rising, the history books scattered on the table, and indirectly the inter-mezzo on the foolscap thing.

However, at twelve he was going to his history coach for an hour, and he allowed himself twenty minutes' relaxation before this. He had watched the porter take his name for making a row in court, so, as the worst he could do was done, there was obviously no reason why he should discontinue making a row, and it was not till the mouthpiece had got sodden and the sides stuck together that he stopped.

The history coach, the Babe confessed, was rather a trial. He lived in dusty, fusty rooms, and he himself was by far the dustiest, fustiest thing in them. During the first lesson the Babe had had with him, he had employed his hands in cleaning his nails with a button-hook, which was, however, better than that he should not clean them at all. On another occasion a spider had dropped down from the ceiling onto the top of his head, and had walked down his nose, and from there had let itself down onto the note-book which he was using. He was short-sighted, and finishing the lesson at that moment and being entirely unconscious of the spider, had shut it up with a bang in the note-book, and the spider was a fleshy spider. The Babe had tried to get Mr. Stewart to coach him, but that gentleman's time was too deeply engaged already. His own work, he said, "like topmost Gargarus," took the morning, and he imagined that neither he nor the Babe would care to meet over history, however romantically treated, in the afternoon, while social calls rendered the evening equally impossible for both of them.

So the Babe went three times a week to Mr. Swotcham of the spider. He was a young don, but the habits of incessant study had early bent his back, bleared his eyes, and given him a weak, nervous man{125}ner. He rarely took any exercise, and even when he did he only walked a little way along the Trumpington Road. Out of his rooms he was like a sheep that had gone astray, and coasted down the streets, keeping close to the houses, as if afraid that, should he launch himself into mid-pavement, he would lose himself irretrievably. He was a member of an occult, some said obscure, club called the Apostles, the members of which met in each other's rooms in a shame-faced manner every Saturday night, though there was really nothing in the least shameful about their proceedings. In theory it was supposed that they set the world straight once a week, but no doubt they lacked practical ability. The Babe, whose varied acquaintance included several members of this Society, used to ask them to dinner on Saturday night, in order to have the pleasure of hearing them excuse themselves at a quarter to ten. The excuse offered was always the same.

"I'm afraid I've got to go round and see a man."

The Babe followed this up by asking who the man was, to which the invariable reply was: "Oh, only a man I know." Then the brutal Babe throwing the mask aside would say: "Oh, you're going to a meeting of the Apostles, aren't you?" Somehow the members seemed rather ashamed of this fact being thus ruthlessly dragged into light, and the Babe in his May week paper had informed the world that the Apostles were the spiritual descendants of the old Hell-Fire Club of Medmenham Abbey, and that their deeds grew darker and darker every year. For the most part they were radical Agnostics, and they disestablished the English Church about once a month. They affected red ties, to show that they disapproved of everything.

Swotcham was not only an eminent Apostle, a sort of Peter among them, but an eminent historian, and the Babe had the sense to attend to what he said. It is true that this morning he watched with overpowering interest the turning over of the leaves of Swotcham's note-book, until the corpse of the fleshy spider was discovered, blotching and staining the articles of the Magna Charta, but when Swotcham had scratched it off with a J nib, his attention wandered no more.

It was a hopelessly wet and sloppy afternoon, the sort of afternoon when everything looks at its worst, and Cambridge worst of all. Grey sheets of rain drifted and drizzled over the Great Court, driven fretfully against the window panes by a cold easterly wind which struck the spray of the fountain beyond the basin out sideways onto the path. Outside the gate, the lime trees wept sooty tears and leaves early-dead, and the asphalt of Trinity Street looked like the surface of some stagnant dirty river, distortedly reflecting the dull-faced houses on each side. A melancholy gurgle of water streamed into the grating in the centre of the so-called Whewell's Court, and its more classical name seemed to be divinely apt. The air was close, cold, and infinitely damp, and two or three terriers inhumanely left outside the Pitt, appeared like a realistic rendering of discomfort personified.

So the judicious Babe betook himself to the smoking room of that club, which always maintains a uniformity of gloom and comfort, whatever the weather is, and thought to himself as he settled in a big armchair that until he left, the weather could have no further depressing influence. He took out of the library the inimitable *Ravenshoe* which he already knew nearly by heart, and read with undiminished enjoyment of how Napoleon and a colonial Bishop whose real name was Jones, gave testimonials to a corn-cutter, who had them printed in his advertisement, and of how Gus and Flora were naughty in church. Later on, he proposed to have hot toast with his tea.

He had not been there long when Reggie came in, and as the Babe was not disposed to talk, and merely grunted when he was sat on, he got out a new book called *Gerald Eversley's Friendship*, and proceeded to read about the peculiarities which mark the boys at St. Anselm's.

A short silence.

"Goozlemy, goozlemy, goozlemy," quoted the Babe.

"Look here, Babe."

"Well."

"Harry Venniker produces from the bottom of his box a quantity of sporting prints, and an enormous stag's head—a 'royal' he called it. Did you ever see a play-box that size?"

"No. There isn't one. 'My dear, there is going to be a collection, and I have left my purse on the piano.' I wish I knew Flora."

Silence.

"'After all, in this life the deepest, holiest feelings are inexpressible.' Oh, I draw the line somewhere—"

"Yes, if you don't draw the line somewhere," murmured the Babe, "where are you to draw the line?"

"Gerald of course sobs violently on getting into bed, the first night at St. Anselm's, and Harry puts his hand on his shoulder, and says he'll be his friend for ever. Then 'Gerald laid his head anew upon the pillow, and was at peace.' Good Lord! This was an 'incident of which the pale moon, throned in heaven, was the sole arbitress.' He says so," shouted Reggie, "and it is a 'study in real life.' He says that too, on the title-page, in capital letters. He says it very loud and plain, several times."

The Babe chuckled comfortably, and shut up *Ravenshoe*.

"I read it yesterday," he said. "Turn on to about page 90 or so. I think you'll find the passage marked in pencil. He has to sing a song in which a swear-word comes, and when he gets to it, he breaks down, hides his face in his hands, and rushes from the hall."

Reggie's eyes grew rounder and rounder.

"So they propose to send him to Coventry for a month."

"That's the place my governor is member for," remarked the Babe, "and they make bicycles there."

"The little brute—aged thirteen, Babe, about as old as you," continued Reggie, "reads books of science (particularly archæology), even sermons and books of controversial divinity, in the college library. If that is real life, give me fiction."

"Quite a little Zola," said the Babe, "our new, harmless, English realist. A little later on a churchyard becomes an element in Gerald's life. Are churchyards elements in your life, Reggie?"

"Yes, of course."

"Later on again," continued the Babe, "he gets in a row for cribbing. The author gets hold of such wonderfully new and original situations. The evidence against him is overwhelming, absolutely overwhelming, and the mystery is never cleared up. As you read, your suspense is only equalled by the suspense of the author. He finds it almost unbearable."

"I can't read any more," said Reggie. "Tell me what happens."

"Oh, all the regular things. Harry gets into the eleven, and Gerald Eversley turns into Robert Elsmere for a time. Then of course he falls in

love with Harry's sister, who gallops away in consumption, and dies. So
Gerald determines to commit suicide, and leaves a note for Harry saying
what he is going to do, and just as he is preparing to jump into a lake—
he has previously thrown his coat with a stone wrapped up in it, into the
water—he feels a hand on his shoulder. It's Harry of course. Naturally he
has found the letter, which tells him that the writer will be a corpse when
he finds it, which is a black lie, and goes off just in time to the place where
Gerald very prudently tells him that the deed will be done. So Gerald goes
to a town in the North of England, probably Coventry again, and wears a
locket of purest enamel, with the name 'Ethel' on it. The book ends: 'He is
dead now.'"

Reggie was still turning over the leaves of the book.

"Who is Mr. Selby?"

"The good young master with a secret sorrow, to whom all the boys
open their hearts."

"I see that Harry lies at death's door, having caught inflammation of the
lungs in a football match. That's another original situation."

"Oh dear, yes, and old gentlemen cannot meet fifty years after they
have left school without saying: 'You remember that catch? My dear fellow,
why did you let that ball go through your legs?' I would sooner be Babe all
my life than live to be an old man like that."

"And Harry gets the last goal just before time. The back's leg 'flashed.'
I've never seen your legs flash, Babe."

"No—I'm only a half-back."

"That accounts for it. Let's have tea, and then we'll play a game of pills."

"All right. Then you can dine in Hall with me. I can't afford dinner in
my room, and we'll work afterwards."

X
Royal Visitors

"Prince and Princess!" he cried. "That means
Will play at being kings and queens." —Hotch-potch
Verses.

Mr. Stewart, as has been indicated before, had a weakness, and that was an amiable and harmless one. His weakness was for the aristocracy. Compared with this, his feeling for royalty which was of the same order, but vastly intensified, might also be called a total failure of power, a sort of mental general paralysis. So when one day towards the middle of August, the wife of the Heir Apparent of a certain European country caused a telegram to be sent to him, to the effect that her Royal Highness wished to visit Cambridge before leaving the country, and would be graciously pleased to take her luncheon with him, Mr. Stewart was naturally a proud man. He bought a long strip of brilliant red carpet, he ordered a lunch from the kitchen that set the mouth of the cook watering, "and altogether," as the Babe very profanely and improperly said, "made as much fuss as if the Virgin Mary had been expected." He also sent printed cards, "to have the honour of," to the Vice-chancellor, the heads of four colleges and their wives, and also to another Fellow of his college, who only a term before, had entertained at tea a regular royal queen, and had asked him to meet her. And remembering that he had once met the Prince of Wales at a dance in London given by the Babe's mother, he also asked the Babe. At the last moment, however, the Princess sent a telegram saying that she was going to bring her husband with her, which would mean two more places, one for him, and one for his gentleman-in-waiting, and Mr. Stewart, whose table would not hold any more than fifteen conveniently, sent a hurried message and apology to the Babe, saying that all this was very upsetting, and unexpected, and uncomfortable, and inconvenient, but that he was sure the Babe would see his difficulty. He would, however, be delighted and charmed if the Babe would come in afterwards, and at least take a cup of coffee, and a cigarette (for the Princess did not mind smoking, and indeed once at Aix-les-Bains he had seen her, etc., etc.), and sun himself in the smile of royalty.

The Babe received this message at half-past one; he had refused an invitation to lunch at King's on the strength of the previous engagement, and he was rather cross. It was too late to go to King's now, but after a few moments' thought, his face suddenly cleared and he sent a note to Reggie saying that he would come round about half-past two, adding that he had "got an idea," which they would work out together. He then ordered some lunch from the kitchen, which there was little chance of his receiving for some time, for all the cooks and kitchen boys who were not engaged in serving up Mr. Stewart's lunch, were busy making little excursions into the court, where they stood about with trays on their heads, to give the impression that they were going to or from some other rooms, in order to catch a sight of Mr. Stewart's illustrious guests as they crossed the court. However, the Babe went to the kitchen himself as it did not come, and said bitter things to the head cook who was a Frenchman, and asked him whether he had already forgotten about Alsace and Lorraine.

He lunched alone and half-way through he nearly choked himself with laughing suddenly, apparently at nothing at all, and when he had finished he went round to King's. He and Reggie talked together for about an hour, and then went out shopping.

Later in the day Mr. Stewart called on the Babe, to express his regret at what had happened, but his regret was largely tempered with sober and loyal exultation at the success of his party. Their Royal Highnesses had been the embodiment of royal graciousness and amiability; they had written their names in his birthday book, and promised to send their photographs. The conversation, it appeared, had been carried on chiefly in French, a language with which Mr. Stewart was perfectly acquainted, and which he spoke not only elegantly, but what is better, intelligibly. The Princess was the most beautiful and delightful of women, the Prince the handsomest and most charming of men. Mr. Stewart, in fact, had quite lost his heart to them both, and he had promised to look them up when he next happened to be travelling in their country, which, thought the cynical Babe, would probably be soon. Best of all, Mr. Medingway, the entertainer of queens, could not talk French, though he was the first Arabic scholar in Europe, a language, however, in which it was not possible for a mixed company to converse, and he had necessarily been quite thrown into the shade.

The Babe received this all with the utmost interest and sympathy. He regretted that he had not been able to come in afterwards, but he hoped Mr. Stewart could come to breakfast next day at nine. Mr. Stewart both could and would, and as soon as he had gone, the Babe danced the *pas-de-quatre* twice round the room.

That evening Reggie and the Babe went to call on Jack Marsden who had come up for a week. Jack was very short, barely five feet high, but he made up for that by being very stout. The Babe also got a fine nib, and employed half an hour in copying something very carefully onto the back of a plain black-edged envelope.

He was up in good time next morning, and he had three letters by the post. One of these was black-edged, and had on the back of the envelope a Royal Crown, and *Windsor Castle*. He opened them all, and left this last face downwards on the table.

Mr. Stewart came in, still in the best of spirits, and walked about the room, expatiating on the superiority of royal families, while the Babe made tea.

"It makes a difference," said Stewart, "it must make a difference, if one's fathers and forefathers have been kings. One would have the habit and the right of command. I don't know if I ever told you—"

His eye caught sight of the Royal Crown and Windsor Castle, and he paused a moment.

"I don't know if I ever told you of that very pleasant day I once spent at Sandringham."

"Yes, you told me about it yesterday," said the Babe brutally.

"I suppose they are all up in Scotland now," said Stewart.

"No, the Queen is at Windsor for a day or two," said the Babe. "She goes up early next week. Will you have a sole?"

"Thanks—not a whole one. I asked because I saw you had a letter here from Windsor."

The Babe looked up quickly and just changed colour—he could do it quite naturally—and picked up his letters.

"Yes, it's from my cousin," he said. "She's in waiting, just now."

"Lady Julia?"

"Yes. Apparently they are not going straight up."

The subject dropped, but a few minutes later the Babe said suddenly and in an absent-minded way.

"I don't think she's ever been to Cambridge before."

"Lady Julia?"

Again the Babe started.

"Yes, Lady Julia. She is thinking of coming up to—to see me on Monday. Is there anything in the papers?"

"I only read the *Morning Post*," said Mr. Stewart. "There is of course a short account of the Prince's visit here, but I saw nothing else."

For the next day or two the Babe was very busy, too busy to do much work. He went more than once with Reggie and Jack to the A.D.C. where they looked up several dresses, and he had a long interview with the proprieter of the Bull. He took a slip of paper to the printer's, with certain elaborate directions, and on Monday morning there arrived at Trinity a Bath chair. Then he went to Mr. Stewart, who was his tutor, and had a short talk, with the result that at a quarter to two, Mr. Stewart was pacing agitatedly up and down his room, stopping always in front of the window, from which he could see the staircase on which were the Babe's rooms, and on which now appeared a long strip of crimson carpet. As luck would have it Mr. Medingway selected this time for going to Mr. Stewart's rooms to borrow a book and the two looked out of the window together.

The Trinity clock had just struck two, when a smart carriage and pair hired from the Bull stopped at the gate, and the Babe's gyp, who had been waiting at the porter's lodge, wheeled the Bath chair up to it. Out of it stepped first the Babe, next a short stout old lady dressed in black, and last a very tall young woman elegantly dressed. She was quite as tall as the Babe, and seemed the type of the English woman of the upper class, who plays lawn-tennis and rides bicycles. The gyp bowed low as he helped the old lady into the chair, and the Babe, hat in hand until the old lady told him to put it on, and the tall girl walked one on each side of it. The porter who was just going into the lodge, stopped dead as they passed, and also took off his hat, and the Bath chair passed down an inclined plane of boards which had been arranged over the steps into the court.

Mr. Stewart, standing with Medingway at his bow window, saw them enter, and in a voice trembling with suppressed excitement said to his companion: "Here they are," and though benedictions were not frequent on his lips, added: "God bless her."

He pressed Medingway to stop for lunch, and the two sat down together.

"Was it in the papers this morning?" asked the latter.

Mr. Stewart took the *Morning Post* from the sofa.

"It is only announced that the Court will leave Windsor to-day. They are expected at Balmoral on Wednesday, not Tuesday, you see. It does not give their movements for to-day."

Mr. Medingway was looking out of the window.

"They have got to the staircase," he said. "And she is getting out. Are we—is anyone going in afterwards?"

"I believe not. It is to be absolutely quiet, and strictly incognito. They leave again by the 4.35."

"An interesting, a unique occasion," said Medingway.

"Yes; the Babe takes it all so easily. I wish I had been able to have him to lunch last week."

Mr. Medingway smiled, and helped himself to a slice of galantine.

"They wouldn't perhaps take a cup of tea before going—"

"Certainly not," said Mr. Stewart, who, if he was not playing the *beau rôle* to-day, at any rate had been in the confidence of him who was. "The Babe was most urgent that I should not let it get about. Indeed, I have committed a breach of confidence in telling you. Of course I know it will go no further."

Meantime, the Babe having successfully conveyed his party across the court, and having taken the precaution of sporting his door, was having lunch. Opposite to him sat Jack Marsden, dressed in a black silk gown; on his right Reggie, attired in the height of fashion. He wore a blue dress with very full sleeves, and a large picture hat. He was taking a long draught of Lager beer.

"Stewart and Medingway both saw," he said, "and they are both at Stewart's window now."

"It was complete," said the Babe solemnly, "wonderfully complete, and the bogus copy of the *Morning Post*, which I substituted for his, was completer still. It will also puzzle them to know how you get away, for they are sure to wait there on the chance of seeing you again. I shouldn't wonder if Stewart went to the station. And now if you've finished, you can change in my bedroom, and we'll go round and get a fourth to play tennis. Stewart must confess that I have gone one better than either him or Medingway."

XI
The Rehearsal

They had a rustic woodland air
—After Wordsworth.

Ealing had not been up in the Long, but Reggie and the Babe spent a week with him early in October, before going up to Cambridge again. They arrived on the last day of September, and from morn till eve on the first day the silly pheasants fled before the Babe's innocuous gun. However, that gentleman said he liked aiming, without any thought of ulterior consequences, and that this was the true essence of sport, and as Reggie and Ealing were both good shots, it is to be presumed that everyone, even including the keeper, was fairly contented.

The October term began as October terms always begin. There was, as usual, a far larger number of Freshmen of unique brilliance than had ever been heard of before, who were duly asked to coffee with men of other years after Hall, and these ceremonies were neither more nor less exciting than usual. There was the Freshman who wore spectacles, and didn't play games because he had a weak heart, and who when asked from what school he came, said 'Giggleswick,' with almost incredible coolness; there was the Freshman who had been captain of the eleven in some obscure school, and already saw himself captain of the University team; there were Freshmen who could play all kinds of music, the Freshman who played the flute, and the Freshman who played the violin, and probably the Freshman who could play the sackbut and psaltery; the Freshman who already seemed to know half the University, and the Freshman who knew nobody at all; the Freshman who called his tutor "Sir," and the Freshman who very kindly treated him as one man of the world treats another. There were the usual trial games of football played under a tropical sun, and the usual interminable lists of tubbings put up in the Reading-Room.

But after a fortnight or so the world in general, with all its sorts and conditions of men, settled down into its usual routine, the Freshmen who had all started together diverged into the sets where their particular tastes attracted them. Some joined musical societies, and some were put up and blackballed at a meeting of the old Giggleswickians; some played in the Freshmen's matches, and some bought college blazers, and passed contented and leisurely afternoons in canoes on the Backs. Alan St. Aubyn published his annual humorous libel on what he playfully called University Life, and the Babe moved from Malcolm Street into the rooms he had occupied in the Long in the Great Court Trinity, and Mr. Sykes signalised the occasion by killing the under-porter's best cat.

No doubt it was primarily the best cat's fault, for she had taken an independent and solitary walk on her own account down Trinity Street, and Sykes who was waiting at the gate, quite quiet and as good as gold, for the Babe, who had gone into his room to put down his cap and gown, saw her returning. So he killed her. Of course he had to tell the Babe about it, and he thought the best plan would be to take the mangled corpse—she was not neatly killed—to the Babe's rooms, which, though he was not allowed in college, he happened to know, and the first thing the porter saw was Mr. Sykes racing across the grass with his best cat hopelessly defunct, dangling from his mouth. He followed, but Sykes got there first, and was wagging his stumpy tail with a pleased air, as he deposited his burden on the hearth-rug, when the infuriated porter entered.

The porter said:

(I.) That Sykes had no business to kill his cat.

(II.) That he had, if possible, even less business in college.

(III.) That Sykes ought to be poisoned.

The Babe answered:

(I.) That there was no question of poisoning Sykes.

(II.) That the death must have taken place outside college, for he had seen Sykes enter with the corpse in his mouth.

(III.) That the cat had no more business in Trinity Street than Sykes had in college, so it was six of one and half a dozen of the other.

(IV.) That Sykes should be beaten.

(V.) That, though the cat was not worth it, sentiment went for something, and there was such a thing as a sovereign.

So Sykes was beaten there and then with a rug strap, and the porter had a sovereign, and the beaten Sykes was granted safe conduct out of college again.

The Babe took a hansom down to the theatre, for he was going to rehearse for the Greek play, and blew tobacco smoke at Sykes all the way to show him he was in disgrace. He had not much wanted to act, for it meant six weeks of rehearsing and learning his part, but he had consented to read through the play and see whether the part of Clytemnestra in the *Agamemnon* did not recommend itself to him. This had of course ended in his undertaking it, and he found that though he had dropped Greek for two years, he did not experience much difficulty in learning his part.

The theatre where the *Agamemnon* was to be performed was a curiously shabby building, resembling an overgrown barn, one of the "greater barns," so said the Babe, mentioned in a parable. A low tunnel, resembling the subway in Metropolitan underground stations led into it from the street, and from the tunnel opened various doors, which led into rooms resembling economically constructed kennels. One of these, humorously called the smoking-room, presumably because the audience invariably smoked in the passage, was rendered additionally alluring by a long, low plank, like those supplied to third class waiting-rooms, which ran down the length of it. The outer wall, in all its unveiled glory of brick and mortar, was further decorated by photographs of the Compton Company, in which actors and actresses alike seemed devoured by a futile endeavour to acquire those casts of expression which are associated with "persons of genius and sensibility." A man was engaged in kindling reluctant footlights when the Babe entered, and he had time to bestow the minutest attention on the very vivid drop-scene which was down, before the others appeared. It represented a gloomy and nameless marsh, in the corner of which was moored a magenta boat, into which a young lady in a green bonnet was being assisted by a young gentleman of abhorrent demeanour and odiously familiar manner. He wore a straw hat and a blue frock-coat, and was smoking an enormous cigar. Over their heads hovered a gigantic bird of prey, probably a vulture, confident no doubt that the fatal exhalations from the marsh, or their own unfitness to live, would soon supply him with a delicate supper composed of the remains of this ill-attired pair. A painted but unexplained Venetian mast—in popular language, a barber's pole—stuck out of the bulrushes in the middle distance, and behind, the sun appeared to have just set in a gory sky over the mountains, which stood up brilliantly blue in the background.

It was a miserably cold morning, and Clytemnestra sat in a thick ulster with a bull-dog on her knees, till it was time for her to appear, and watched a curiously dressed chorus of Argive elders headed by Reggie in flannels and a blazer, for he had been playing tennis, manœuvre round a stage director, whom a vivid imagination construed into an altar. Two other stage directors quarrelled with each other in the background, till the conductor who was directing the chorus asked them to be quiet. Thus he secured for himself the hostility of all the stage directors, who resented the attack made on their class, and who lay in wait to contradict him rudely on the earliest possible occasion.

The Babe, meantime, had wandered off the stage into the wings, in search of a fire, and Mr. Sykes, left to himself, recognised Reggie as a friend among the heterogeneous elders, and trotted across to him, wheezing pathetically. The conductor had stopped the chorus in order to point out some mistake the tenors had made, and was singing the passage himself in a fruity falsetto voice, and Reggie, who was a bass, was patting Sykes, when the voice of one of the hostile stage directors broke in—

"The rehearsal," he said firmly, "will proceed when the leader of the Argive elders has quite finished playing with a bull-dog. Please send the bull-dog out of the theatre."

"It's Clytemnestra's," said Reggie.

The Babe re-appeared at this moment.

"Where's Bill?" he asked. "Oh, there he is. Come here, darling. Oh, are you waiting for me?"

The conductor laid down his baton.

"Settle it among yourselves," he said, "and tell me when you are ready. I may remark that I am very busy, and that my time is not my own."

Mr. Sykes meantime was sniffing suspiciously round the heels of the altar, and the altar was getting visibly nervous.

The Babe supposing that his entrance had come, began reciting his first lines in a loud voice, and the stage directors and the conductors made common cause against him.

"If Clytemnestra would kindly be quiet," said one.

"And take away her horrible dog," put in the altar.

"The chorus might proceed," shouted the conductor.

The Babe with a look of injured innocence on his face retired to his chair, followed reluctantly by Sykes, who was not satisfied about the altar, and the practice went on.

But the truce between the conductor and the stage directors was only an armed neutrality. One of them in particular, a bustling little man with a honey-coloured moustache and a Paderewski head of hair, was waiting to fall upon him. He was a student of all branches of what Stewart would have called "delightful and useless knowledge"; on such subjects he has perhaps a wider and more elaborately specialised information than any man in England. He could have told you with the most minute particulars the exact shape of the earrings worn by Greek women of the fifth century B.C., the particular way in which athletes of the fourth century brushed their hair, the conformation of the lobe of the ear in female statues of the third century, or the proportionate length of the little finger nail to the eye-socket in bronzes of the Hadrian epoch. He could have prescribed you the ingredients which made the red in Botticelli's Tobias, lasting, through the want of which Turner's sunsets paled almost as fast as the sunsets themselves; he had penetrated into the dens of the forgers at Rome which lie in the street which no one can find between the Via Nazionale and the Capitol; he had been twice round the world, and spoke five dialects of Mexican; he had looked on the city of Mecca, and kodaked the interior of the mosque of the Seven Curses of the Prophet; he had dived for pearls in the Coromandel Sea, and evaded by a hair-breadth the jaws of the blue-nosed shark as it rolled over on its back to snap him in two; he knew intimately a lineal descendant of Adamo di Brescia, the coiner of the Inferno, and asserted that in all probability the forefather was a clumsier workman than his son, or he would never have been detected. And on all these subjects and many others equally abstruse he could give you statistics, as dry as the facts themselves were interesting. Once or twice, it is true, he had been caught in an apparent error, but he had always been able to give a perfectly satisfactory explanation of it afterwards, with hardly any time for reflection. Such qualifications had eminently fitted him for the part of stage-manager in a Greek play, and he certainly added to these, immense zeal and industry. His name was Propert, and his college was Peterhouse.

For some minutes he stood grasping his hair with both hands in an incipient frenzy, as the chorus proceeded, but at last he could stand it no longer, and he clapped his hands loudly.

"It is all wrong," he said, "you have not got the spirit of it. You do not sound the note of fate. Those last bars should be a long low wail, prophetic of woe, and *pianissimo—pianissimo ma con smorgando tremuloso.*"

He patted the air in front of Reggie, with an eloquent gesture.

"They are marked *ff.*," said the leader of the Argive elders in good plain English.

"Well, you must erase your double forte," said Dr. Propert.

The conductor folded his arms, and waited till Dr. Propert had retired up O. P.

"We will now begin again four bars back, at the double forte," he remarked.

"Yes, *pianissimo,*" said the doctor turning round.

The Argive elders looked puzzled. Diplomacy, to judge by their speeches, was not their strong point.

"Are we to do it double forte or *pianissimo*?" asked Reggie of the conductor.

"I presume that Doctor Propert has informed Professor Damien of the alterations he has thought fit to make in the music," he remarked bitterly.

But as Doctor Propert was already employed in showing Agamemnon, who was about to enter, how to lean against a door in the attitude of a Sophoclean adult, the sarcasm fell innocuous, and the practice proceeded *fortissimo* without further interruption.

Agamemnon had forgotten his first line, and at Dr. Propert's suggestion said "Boble, boble, boble," until he remembered the second or third lines, and the chorus grouped themselves round the watchmen and smoked, while the altar, relieved of its localising duties, quarrelled with the other unemployed directors, and prompted Agamemnon intermittently.

But as the scene between Agamemnon and Clytemnestra proceeded and the Babe warmed to his work, other conversation drooped and died. He found it bored him simply to say the part, and throughout the rehearsals, even when he had to read his part, he acted it all. But at this stage in rehearsal he knew it by heart, and in looking at him one quite forgot his deerstalker cap and long, loud ulster. The stage directors were reconciled and murmured approbation, the conductor ceased talking to the watchmen, and the thing began to take shape. Even the subsequent appearance of Mr. Sykes, who sat down in the middle of the stage and smiled at the chorus, caused no interruption. He fell perfectly flat, and no one took the slightest notice of him.

Once only was there an interruption, and that was made by the Babe himself. Dr. Propert was busy hauling a metope on to the stage, and letting go of it for a moment, it fell resonantly onto its back. The Babe stopped dead, and turned round.

"If you make such a horrible row again, while I'm on," he said, "you may take the part of Clytemnestra yourself. I shall begin again," he added severely, "at the beginning of my speech."

The conductor could have embraced the Babe on the spot, and the other stage managers giggled. The Babe waited till they had quite finished, and then began again thirty-four lines back.

The truth was that all the Babe's flippancy and foolishness left him when he was acting, and only then, for acting was the one thing he took quite seriously. He ceased to be himself, for he threw himself completely into the character he was impersonating. He was in fact not an amateur, but an actor, and these two have nothing whatever to do with one another. If a man has dramatic power, he may become an actor with training, without it he cannot. And most amateurs have not got it.

So the play proceeded with vigour till Clytemnestra went off with Ægisthus, and shortly after in a hansom with Mr. Sykes. The cold drizzle of the morning had turned to snow, and the melting snow in the streets looked like thin coffee ice. The Babe was playing in a college match that afternoon, and the prospect filled him with a mild despair.

XII
A College Sunday

"This gloomy tone," he said, "is far too rife;
I'll demonstrate the loveliness of life." —Hotch-potch
Verses.

Reggie and Ealing had moved into a set of rooms in Fellows' Buildings, which they shared together. The set consisted of three rooms, two inner and smaller ones, and one large room looking out on to the front court of King's. The two smaller rooms they used as bedrooms, but as they each had folding Eton beds, by half-past nine or so every morning, provided that they got up in reasonable time, they were converted for the day into sitting-rooms. The outer room was furnished more with regard to what furniture they had, than what furniture it required. Thus there were two pianos, tuned about a quarter of a tone apart from each other, two grandfather's clocks, and a most deficient supply of chairs. "However," as Reggie said, "one can always sit on the piano."

Ealing's powers of execution on the piano were limited. He could play hymn-tunes, or other compositions, where the next chord to the one he was engaged on followed as a corollary from it, and anything in the world which went so slowly as to enable him to glance from the music to his hands between each chord, however complicated it was, provided it did not contain a double sharp, which he always played wrong. He could also, by dint of long practice, play "Father O'Flynn" and the first verse of "Off to Philadelphia in the Morning"; and there seemed to be no reason why, with industry, he should not be able to acquire the power of playing the other verses, in which he considered the chords to be most irregular and unexpected, deserting the air at the most crucial points. Reggie, however, was far more accomplished. He had got past hymn-tunes. The Intermezzo in *Cavaleria Rusticana*—even the palpitating part—was from force of repetition mere child's play to him, and he aspired to the slow movements out of Beethoven's Sonatas.

The hours in which each might practise, therefore, demanded careful arrangement. College regulations forbade the use of the pianos altogether between nine in the morning, and two in the afternoon, since it was popularly supposed by the authorities who framed this rule—and who shall say them nay—that all undergraduates worked between these hours, and that the sound of a piano would disturb them. Consequently, Ealing was allowed to play between eight A.M. and nine A.M., every morning, a privilege which he used intermittently during breakfast, and by which he drove Reggie, daily, to the verge of insanity, and Reggie between two P.M. and three P.M. Ealing again might play between three and five, and Reggie from five to seven. During these hours the temporary captain of the pianos, even if he did not wish to play himself, might stop the other from playing except with the soft pedal down. It had been found impossible to regulate the hours after dinner, and they often played simultaneously on their several pianos, and produced thereby very curious and interesting effects, which sounded Wagnerian at a sufficient distance. Finally, the use of the piano was totally prohibited by common consent between two A.M. and eight A.M.

The Babe, like mournful Œnone, "hither came at noon" one Sunday morning. Chapel at King's was at half-past ten, and that English habit of mind which weds indissolubly together Sunday morning and lying in bed, was responsible for the fact that on Sunday Reggie and Ealing always breakfasted after chapel. But the Babe, unlike that young lady, was in the best of spirits, and as Ealing and Reggie were not yet back from chapel, made tea and began breakfast without them. They came in a few minutes later, both rather cross.

"When there is going to be a sermon," said Reggie severely, taking off his surplice, "I consider that I have a right to be told. Morning, Babe."

"Oh, have you had a sermon?" said the Babe sweetly. "Who preached?"

"The Dean. He preached for half-an-hour."

"More than half-an-hour," said Ealing. "Totally inaudible, of course, but lengthy to make up for that."

"Pour me out some tea, Babe, if you've had the sense to make it."

"Sermons are trying if one hasn't breakfasted," said the Babe. "They are sermons in stones when one asks for bread."

"What do you mean?"

"I haven't the slightest idea. I hoped that perhaps one of you would know. Why should I know what I mean? It's other people's business to find out. And they for the most part neglect it shamefully."

"Shut up, Babe," growled Reggie. "I wish you wouldn't talk when I'm eating."

"Can't you hear yourself eat?" asked the Babe sympathetically.

"Wild horses shall not drag me to Chapel this afternoon," said Ealing. "We'll go for a walk, Reggie."

"I daresay: at present I can't think of anything but food. Babe, you greedy hog, give me some fish."

"And very good fish it is," said the Babe genially. "By the way, Sykes is far from well this morning."

"What's the matter with him?"

"He partook too freely of the anchovies of the Chitchat last night. You will find that in French conversation books."

"I saw him indulging as I thought unwisely," said Ealing. "Then it was surely imprudent of him to drink Moselle cup."

"He wished to drown care, but it only gave him a stomach-ache. Stewart impressed him so with the fact that we were all Atlases with the burden of the world on our shoulders, that he had recourse to the cup."

"And the burden of us all was on Stewart."

"Yes. Don't you remember he said that he felt personally responsible for every undergraduate whom he had ever spoken to? His idea is that each don ought to have an unlimited influence, and that the whole future of England in the next generation lay on each of them, particularly himself. No wonder his eyelids were a little weary, as Mr. Pater says. But after you went he took the other side, and said that the undergraduates were the *raison d'être* of the University, and that the dons existed only by their sufferance."

"Did Longridge stop?"

"Yes. He was a little less coherent than usual. I know he took the case of a man at Oxford who threw stones at the deer in Magdalen, though what conclusion he drew from it, I can't say."

"Probably that the deer were really responsible for the undergraduates."

The Babe sighed.

"I have to read a paper next week. I think it shall be on some aspects of Longridge. That is sure to give rise to a discussion if he is there. Give me a cigarette, Reggie."

The Babe established himself in a big chair by the fireplace, while the others finished breakfast.

"I am going to found a club," he said, "called the S.C.D. or Society for the Cultivation of Dons. Stewart says he will be vice-president, as he doesn't consider himself a don. We are going to call on obscure dons every afternoon and speak to them of the loveliness of life, for, as Stewart says, the majority of them have no conception of it. Their lives are bounded by narrow horizons, and the only glimpse they catch of the great world, is their bed-maker as she carries out their slop-pail from their bedrooms. They live like the Niebelungs in dark holes and eat roots, and though they are merely animals, they have no animal spirits. He says he knew a don once who by a sort of process of spontaneous combustion, became a dictionary, but all the interesting words, the sort of words one looks out in a Bible dictionary, you know, were missing. So they used him to light fires with, for which he was admirably adapted, being very dry, and in the manner of King Alexander, who, as Stewart asserted, became the bung in a wine cork, other dons now warm themselves at him. Stewart was very entertaining last night, and rather improper. He said that a Don Juan or two was wanted among the dons, by way of compensation, and he enlarged on the subject."

"Give us his enlargements."

"I can't. He enlarged in a way that belongs to the hour after midnight on Saturday, when you know that when you wake up it will be Sunday. He was very Saturday-night. He called it working off the arrears of the week, and complained that he hadn't heard a mouth-filling oath for more than a month. He never swears himself, but he likes to hear other people do it; for he says he is in a morbid terror of the millennium beginning without his knowing it. He skipped about in short skirted epigrams, and pink-tight phrases. At least that was his account of his own conversation when we parted. Oh yes, and he said he didn't mind saying these things to me because I was a man of the world."

"He knows your weak points, Babe," said Reggie.

"Not at all. He referred to that as my strong point."

"Good old Clytemnestra! I'm better now, thank you, after my breakfast, and it's 'The Sorrows of Death' this afternoon. I shall go to chapel again."

Reggie lit a pipe, and picked out the first few bars on the piano.

"The watchman was a tiresome sort of man to have about," he said. "When they asked him if it was nearly morning, he only said, 'Though the morning will come, the night will come also.' Of course they knew that already, and besides it wasn't the question. I should have dismissed him on the spot. So the soprano has to tell them, which he does on the top A mainly."

"When I was a child I could sing the upper upper Z," said the Babe fatuously. "Then my voice broke, and the moral is 'Deeper and deeper yet.' Don't rag: I apologise."

Ealing finished breakfast last, and strolled across to the window.

"It's a heavenly morning," he said. "Let's go out. We needn't go far."

"I will walk no further than the King's field," said the Babe.

"Very well, and we can sit outside the pavilion. I'm lunching out at half-past one."

"Meals do run together so on Sunday. Sunday is really one long attack of confluent mastication," said the Babe. "It's a pity one can't take them simultaneously."

Though November had already begun, the air was deliciously warm and mild, and had it not been for the fast yellowing trees, one would have guessed it to be May. But there was a shouting wind overhead, which stripped off the leaves by hundreds and blew the rooks about the sky. Already the tops of the trees were bare, and the nests of last spring swung empty and half ruined high up among the forks of the branches. During the last week a good deal of rain had fallen, and the Cam was swirling down, yellow and turbid. The willow by the river was already quite bare, and its thin feathery branches lashed themselves against the stone coping of the bridge.

They went through the Fellows' gardens, for Reggie by some means had got hold of a key; there a few bushes of draggled Michaelmas daisies were making pretence that the summer was not quite dead yet, but they only succeeded in calling attention to the long, desolate beds. The grass was growing rank and matted under the autumn rains, and little eddies of leaves had drifted up against the wires of the disused croquet-hoops. But the day itself seemed stolen from off the lap of spring, and two thrushes were singing in the bushes after an excellent breakfast of succulent worms.

"We play you to-morrow at Rugger," remarked the Babe as they walked across the field, "and we play on this ground. It's sticky enough, and I shall vex the soul of the half opposite me, because I like a sticky ground, and he is certain not to. In fact," said he confidently, "I purpose to get two tries off my own bat, and generally to sit on this royal and ancient foundation."

"The Babe has never yet been called modest," said Ealing.

"If I have, I am not aware of it," said the Babe.

"We've got three blues," remarked Reggie.

"I am delighted to hear it," said the Babe. "You will need them all. And you may tell our mutual friend Hargreave that if he attempts to collar me round the ancles again, I shall make no efforts whatever to avoid kicking him in the face. He did it last time we played you, and I spoke to him about it more in sorrow than in anger."

"Upon which the referee warned you for using sorrowful language."

"He did take that liberty," conceded the Babe. "Let's sit down outside the pavilion. I wish we could kick about. The Sabbath is made for man, and so is Sunday, and so are footballs."

"But on Sunday the pavilion is locked up by man, and the footballs put inside."

"It appears so. English people take Sunday too seriously, just as they take everything else, except me."

"Anyhow, Stewart says you are a man of the world," said Ealing.

"He does, and who are we to contradict him? Good Lord, there's one o'clock striking. I must go home. There's somebody coming to lunch at half-past. Reggie, get me a ticket for King's this afternoon, will you?"

XIII
King's Chapel

Music, when soft voices die,
Vibrates in the memory.
Shelley.

Reggie and the Babe got into chapel just after the voluntary had begun, and slow soft notes came floating drowsily down from the echoes in the roof. The chapel and ante-chapel were both full, and from the door in the dim, mellow half-darkness, a sea of heads stretched up to the black wooden screen, through which streamed the light from the chapel itself. In the roof one could just see the delicate fan-shaped lines of vaulting springing across like lotus leaves from wall to wall, and the windows on the south side gleamed with dark, rich colour from the sky already turning red with the southwestern setting sun. As they went up the ante-chapel the Babe saw a seat still unoccupied, and preferred stopping there to going into the chapel.

Reggie's seat was just east of the choir opposite to the window representing Christ standing in the garden after the resurrection. To the right kneels Mary Magdalene gaudily dressed, just having turned and seeing that he was not, as she supposed, only the gardener. To the left rises a green hill, on the top of which, below a row of brown, ragged rocks, stands the empty tomb, with the women round it. By a quaint but curiously felicitous idea of the artist, the figure of Christ is holding a spade in his hand, as if to give colour to Mary's mistake. His face is Divine, but graciously human, and he waits for the recognition.

The whole place had an air of tranquil repose, of remoteness from worldliness, hurry, and unprofitable strivings that perhaps has a certain value, which is not necessarily diminished because it is impossible to account for it statistically or categorically. There is something in spacious grey buildings and perfect Gothic architecture, shared too by broad grass lawns and studious, quiet places and uneventful lives, that cannot be altogether left out of the reckoning when one adds up the total value of a University as compared with a modern endowed plan of education, or the admirable schemes of University extension.

And the choir which walked slowly up the aisle into their places, though composed of ordinary little boys, lay clerks, and undergraduates, somehow brought themselves into harmony with it. On week days the little boys no doubt were entirely human, and probably concealed surreptitious sweet stuff in their pockets; the lay clerks wore bowler hats and tail coats, and belonged to the most unprepossessing class which England produces, and the undergraduates were only undergraduates. But for the time they were part of a wonderful idea, and were performing the office set apart for them by a royal founder.

The last echo from the roof died away, and the service began, and though Reggie was not conscious of attending very closely to it, he was still aware of the good and kindly atmosphere about him, an atmosphere which soothed and quieted, and drove the thoughts inward. He had often felt it before, on other winter afternoons in chapel, and as far as he knew, for he did not consciously think about it, it had made no difference to him. But as no impression is without its effects, we must presume that it had made a difference to him, though he had not been aware of it.

Not long before, the organ had been repaired, and in great part renewed, and it was worthy of its surroundings and its appearance. Golden sheaves of pipes gleamed out between the dark wooden case, and on top of the two turrets looking west, stood two great angels with brazen trumpets to their mouths, and when the "tuba" speaks, one cannot help imagining that it is their trumpets which are sounding. To-day "The Lord thundered out of heaven," and one could think that the air for a moment grew thick with sound, which increased till it shattered the growing darkness, splitting it with lightning made audible.

By the end of the Psalms it had grown quite dark outside, and the windows showed black between the delicate tracery. From the lectern came the story of Nebuchadnezzar's dream, "of the watcher and the Holy One," and afterwards of the Holy One who watched alone among the olives in the Garden of Gethsemane, a king, not of Babylon, but of the whole earth, who had not where to lay his head.

The stalls and sub-stalls were all full of members of the college, in surplices, but the black crowd beyond stretched up to the steps of the altar, and when the three bars of introduction to the solo began, every one stood up. Mendelssohn, so often only correct, so often ruined by his fatal prettiness, has here struck the right note, full and firm. Even Reggie ceased to think of the evasiveness of the watchman, and only listened, till the repeated call of the minor died away into a long pause before the soprano answered, and the choir took up the full chorus.

Outside in the ante-chapel, though only for a little while, the Babe ceased from his customary futility of thought, and the slow opening of the carved wooden doors in the screen, and the drawing of the crimson curtain, at the end of service, still found him meditative.

As the choir came out, framed in a long shaft of light, the organ was played quietly, and then paused for a moment, while a great pedal note made the air shake and quiver in sensation rather than sound. Then the full organ burst out with the *Occasional Overture*, as the congregation from the chapel streamed out after the members of the college. The first movement marched, and marching marshalled whole armies of sound, which stood waiting while the second rippled and laughed and sang with all the breezes of heaven behind it, and the third dwelt dreamily on what had gone, and thought of what was to come.

Then in the last movement, battalion after battalion of major chords, from choir and swell and great organ, grew and multiplied in all their forces, the flutes and piccolos, the twelfths and fifteenths as flying squadrons on the wings, and the diapasons the lords of sound in the centre, an exceeding great army. Then at the second repeat the "tuba" woke in the "huge house of sounds," and the thing was complete, a fixed star for ever in the heavens of harmony.

XIV
A Variety Entertainment

In truth
I know of noone so adaptable.
Old Play.

That evening the Babe dined as a guest with the T.A.F. (which means Twice A Fortnight, and is a synonym for O.A.W. or Once A Week, and implies a frankly purposeless and purely social club consisting of about a dozen members, chiefly undergraduates, who dined together every Sunday night) and spent a pleasant evening of innocent mirth and a little music. After dinner one member sang some Scotch songs in a baritone voice, another played the Pilgrim's March in *Tannhäuser* exceedingly badly, omitting the Venus motif, but repeating the Chorus in a palpitating manner in the higher octave, to make up for it, and two others recalled to their minds the *Occasional Overture* which had been played in chapel that afternoon. A fifth imitated in the most natural and life-like manner the speech and manners of a don of the college, three or four read books gloomily in corners, being of a more serious turn of mind, and the wilder section of the party pressed the Babe to give them a little skirt-dancing, which he very properly refused to do, feeling justly enough that it would not be in keeping with the general character of the proceedings. Later he very unwisely offered to play picquet with anybody, a proposition which was received in awkward silence, and hurriedly covered with a buzz of conversation. Another guest, however, contributed to the harmony of the evening by describing at great length, the state of the lower classes in Russia, Germany, Austria, and Turkey in Asia, with realistic and revolting details. By degrees the other members of the party left their books and their music, and sat round him in enthusiastic silence. For so stirring a man, so thought the Babe, there was no excuse and no hope, for he was not less than thirty years old, and should have known better. Then he reverted, also at length, to the vastly superior conditions of our own agricultural labourers and proceeded, still monologising, by easy transitions, to the prospect of an European war. On this point his prophecies were most patriotic, and went perfectly to the tune of "Rule Britannia," and so afforded everyone present the greatest satisfaction when they reflected that they were Englishmen. Metaphorically speaking he slapped them on the back, and filled them full of roast beef and racial admiration. All his sentiments were worthy of the highest praise, and it may only have been the personality of the speaker that inspired the Babe with such speechless horror. He was just describing the apparatus for shooting torpedoes from submerged tubes on the *Majestic*, which, in some obscure manner the passport of Prince Niktivoffski, which he happened to have about him, had enabled him to inspect, and was saying that no other nation had got anything of the kind and that they would blow all other navies of the world into a million of atoms in a moment of time, when the breaking point came for the Babe, and he rose and said good-night.

He had not got more than half way across the court, when he heard other sounds of revelry from some rooms on the right, belonging as he knew to a don of his acquaintance, who was widely and justly famed for his Sunday evenings at home, and the pleasure-seeking Babe determined to go in for a few minutes, for like the rest of the University, he had a standing invitation to come as often as he could. He found himself in a luxuriously furnished room, quite full of people and of mixed tobacco smoke. His host greeted him effusively, and gave him to understand that his cup of happiness was now quite full.

The gathering was meant to be, and succeeded in being, altogether heterogeneous, and though eminently respectable, had a curious but unmistakable flavour of ultra-Bohemianism about it. Mr. Swotcham was sitting on the sofa near the fire talking excitedly to two shaggy individuals, whom the Babe rightly guessed to be members of the club, which he had libellously informed the world was the modern representative of the Hell-fire Club of Medmenham Abbey. He smiled benignantly at Swotcham, and as he turned away caught the words "standpoint of determinism." He had not the slightest idea what they meant, but they sounded bad. By the table, nibbling biscuits and helping themselves to tea out of a brass Russian samovar, were standing three little men, with little moustaches, talking earnestly together, whose only characteristic seemed to be entire ineffectiveness. Further on a highly-coloured Italian was expressing fervid thoughts in bad English, to two young gentlemen who wore their hair in a great frizzled tuft over their foreheads. This latter type was familiar to the Babe, and afforded him almost infinite delight; it went to the stalls in the theatre, where, dressed in Norfolk jackets, it talked together in dark allusiveness of music-hall *artistes*. It might also be seen in the streets, in a very short and ragged gown, a broken-backed cap with the cardboard showing at the edges, not the result of age, but of fell and evil design, smoking pipes. It gave the world to understand that it was the very devil of a type, but the world, with a charity that is rare, considered that though odious, it was not morally so black as its self-depreciation led it to paint itself.

Arundel prints hung on the walls, and somehow looked as incongruous there as Mrs. Chant at a music-hall, for the whole atmosphere was quite extraordinarily secular. Against the wall stood three or four large bookcases, on the top of which were arranged several admirable reproductions of antique bronzes and marbles. In one corner on the top of a scagliola pedestal stood the bust of the young Augustus in marble, and close to him a bronze Narcissus leaned and held up a listening finger. On each side of the clock on the mantel-piece was a nude figure of a youth in bronze, and Botticelli's Madonna of the Magnificat looked down at them in mild surprise and seemed to be wondering to what sort of a place she had come. From a door on the right came the sounds of the slow movement of Beethoven's *Sonata Pathétique*, arranged not as the composer mean it to be played, but for a cello, a violin and a piano; the piano was a little ahead, but the violin and cello which were running neck to neck, caught up to it in the scherzo that followed, and they all finished up amid indescribable indifference on the part of all present, a dead heat. Everyone talked loudly during the performance, and took not the slightest notice when it was over, with the exception of the genial host, who patted all three executants on the back and said "Awfully jolly, Charlie," to the cellist. The duty of a good host, without doubt, is to make everybody talk, and certainly the musicians and Mr. Waddilove between them succeeded to admiration. The latter was as ubiquitous and as deft as Mr. Maskelyne's hands when he is spinning plates, now giving a touch to the discussion on the standpoint of determinism, now spurring the Italian on to fresh deeds of violence towards the Queen's English, now telling the Babe how he too, in his earlier years, once acted Clytemnestra with unparalleled success, and now persuading Charlie to give him another taste of his cello. In fact, the only group he did not speak to was that of the three earnest biscuit-nibblers, who had been joined by a fourth, and who appeared to be of no consequence whatever, as indeed they were not.

Beyond the room where the music was going on, lay another smaller one, entirely lined with bookcases from floor to ceiling. In one corner stood a screen, and the Babe having the curiosity to peep over it, saw behind, Mr. Waddilove's bed, presided over by a bronze reproduction of the head of "Sleep" from the British Museum. On the table stood a liqueur decanter containing a pale pink fluid of which the Babe took a glass. It reminded him vaguely of almonds and orange peel dissolved in cherry blossom scent, and Mr. Waddilove entering at the moment told him it was made exclusively on the estate of Count Zamboletto near Taormina in Sicily, where he himself had often stayed.

Fresh arrivals kept streaming in; among them two or three members of the T.A.F., who wandered about looking as if they did not know why they had come, including the performer of the overture to *Tannhaüser*, who sat down at the piano, without being asked, and did it again. He appeared to rouse little or no enthusiasm, and left immediately afterwards.

In the music-room the President of the Union had got hold of Mr. Waddilove for a moment, and was discussing the sanitary arrangements of the Union with him, and particularly whether it was possible to stop the thefts of nail-scissors which went on so extensively in the lavatory, and which for no explicable reason, he was inclined to hold the Indians responsible for. He thought that perhaps they collected them, in order to barter with them among savage tribes when they went home. Mr. Waddilove seemed to take but a faint interest in these petty larcenies, but humourously suggested that they should employ some lady bicyclists from Slater's detective agency to see if they could catch the thieves. That failing, he suggested that they should try chaining the scissors to the table or to the looking-glass, after the manner of Bibles in old churches. Close beside them stood the Senior Wrangler of the last year, talking Psychical Research with the sub-organist of Trinity. An archdeacon, who looked like a sheep that had gone very badly astray, was turning over the pages of Max Nordau's *Degeneration*, and close to him an undergraduate, with eyebrows meeting over his nose and the face of a truculent rabbit, was demonstrating the absurdity of the Christian Faith to two frightened Freshmen, who seemed willing to agree to anything he might suggest. As the Babe passed, he heard the words "so-called Resurrection," and his smile grew a shade more seraphic.

The Babe wandered back to the outer room, where the discussion on the standpoint of determinism or some similar subject was still proceeding shrilly. Mr. Swotcham for the moment had the ear of the house, and he was speaking rapidly and excitedly in a sort of cracked treble voice, and apparently endeavouring to tie his fingers into hard knots. They had been joined by three more disputants whom the Babe conjectured to be in the running for the Apostles, for the other three evidently regarded them as promising amateurs rather than professionals.

He made his way across to the window, where he saw Mr. Stewart sitting with a somewhat isolated air.

"This is a very interesting sight, Babe," he said, "and I was looking out for someone to whom I could talk about it. I feel a trifle like St. Anthony in the desert, with all sorts of half-understood temptations beckoning to me. On one side I hear the siren voice of philosophy calling me to leave the world, and live in the realms of pure theory; on the other side of the table stand three joyous Freshmen in the heyday of youth and animal spirits drinking whisky and water, and a fourth, with a temerity which I envy, a curious pink liqueur; on the right you may observe two members of the Footlights Club, who are slaves, so they tell each other, to their divine mistress, Art, to whom they offer sacrificial burlesques twice a year. An archdeacon, with the face of a mediæval saint from a painted glass window, has just gone through into the next room, where he will hear a pupil of mine preaching atheism—"

"I heard someone just now allude to the 'so-called Resurrection.'"

"The chances are a thousand to one that that was he," said Stewart. "Just behind you an Italian is singing the joys of the back streets of Naples to two tuft-haired absurdities, who are sighing to see a little 'life.' Meantime, through the open door I can hear our sub-organist playing the overture to *Parsifal*. He thinks that if he goes on long enough and plays loud enough the conversation will get a little lower. He is wrong. The louder he plays, the louder will everybody talk. In fact he is laying up for them all a store of sore throats to-morrow morning. And our host, whose moral digestion most surely resembles that of an ostrich, turns from one to another, and is appropriate to all. There was also a member of the Upper House here just now, but he did not stop. He had mistaken the character of the entertainment and had come in evening clothes like you, but unlike you had brought his wife décolletée. His entry was pompous, his exit precipitous. As for you, I have long ceased to be surprised at anything you do. But do tell me why you are here?"

The Babe looked round appreciatively.

"I don't know, I'm sure. I came here because I had been dining at the T.A.F. in King's."

"Ah, purely antidotal," said Mr. Stewart.

"Not consciously; and I stopped, I suppose, because it amused me. Surely that is a very good reason."

"The best of reasons, my dear Babe. And when it ceases to amuse you, you will go away, and I will come with you. And I came because it was Sunday, and here one can shake off the impression that it is Sunday, though I don't know why one should be able to do so with such conspicuous success as one does. Somehow in my own rooms everything looks different on Sunday and in consequence they are hardly habitable. I suppose it is the influence of heredity: the rooms are accustomed to generations of dons who always wear black coats on Sundays, and have a cold lunch. Ah, here is the archdeacon. I suppose he has been getting his mind out of its Sunday clothes too. Archdeacons are venerable, are they not? How do you address them, 'Your Veneration' or 'Your Venerance'? Your uncle is a Dean, is he not, Babe? Don't you know?"

"I think it's 'Your Veneree,'" said the Babe, "on the analogy of referee. Look, he's talking to the 'so-called Resurrection.'"

"Then he is probably learning a thing or two," said Mr. Stewart. "That young man never comes to see me without instructing me on the whole duty of a tutor, which appears to be, to do what one intolerable undergraduate tells him. For he is intolerable, neither more nor less. I think I have never met a young man who inspired me with a more searching abhorrence."

The Babe looked at his watch.

"I suppose I shall be gated if I don't go back to Trinity soon," he said.

"It is not unlikely. I will come with you. I am drunk with impressions, and I want a little moral soda-water. As we walk, Babe, you shall speak to me of Rugby football, and drop kicks. That I hope will restore my equilibrium. I understand now why you play football; hitherto it has been a mystery to me. It must be very calming to the moral nature. So tell me what a Punt is."

XV
Clytemnestrismos

Thy warrior comes in regal state,
What words of welcome for him, wife?
The lips of love, the heart of hate,
The bath, the net, the knife.
Stories of Mycenæ.

Between his own tripos work, which he stuck to steadily and grimly, and found by mere force of routine less disagreeable than he expected, Rugby football, the storm and stress of social duties, as he called them—which meant dining out or having people to dinner five nights out of the seven—and constant rehearsals for the Greek play, the Babe's time was very fully taken up. Furthermore, on Mr. Gladstone's principle, though otherwise their principles had nothing in common, he always slept for eight and a half hours every night, and if, as often happened, he did not go to bed till two, the hours of the morning were somewhat curtailed. The Babe, however, did not object to this, as the morning seemed to him the really disagreeable part of the day. There was something crude and raw about the air until lunch-time, which made itself felt, whatever one was doing. It was necessary of course to get through the morning in order to arrive at the afternoon, but the shorter it was made the better, and by breakfasting late and lunching early one could make it very short indeed.

He worked at the Greek play with extraordinary zeal and perseverance. The happy band of directors had begun to see that he knew more about acting than all the rest of them put together, though one had seen two hundred and thirty-seven different French plays, mostly improper, and the Babe was present throughout every rehearsal, sitting in the stalls when he was not on the stage himself, and making suggestions whenever they occurred to him. Mr. Mackay, the second stage director, had very strong and original ideas on the subject of Cassandra, whom he made his special care, and he had mapped out exceedingly carefully the gestures, tones, postures, and faces she was to make as the prophetic afflatus gradually gained possession over her. She was a tall young gentleman with a most lovely girlish face, and about as much knowledge of the dramatic art as of the lunar theory. But Mackay was indefatigable in coaching her. She was to point down with both hands outstretched on the word "blood"; she was to roll her eyes and stare at the centre of the fourth row of stalls at the word "Apollo"; she was to make a noise in her throat resembling gargling on the second "Alas"; she was to stagger on the third, and palpitate on the fourth. She was to gaze with agonised questioning at the Ophicleide when Clytemnestra told her she was mad, as if to ask whether he too agreed with her, and breathe as if she had just come to the surface after a prolonged dive; and from that point onwards she was to cast restraint to the winds. She was mad; let the audience know it. Mad people were incoherent and throaty; what she said was incoherent, let her mode of saying it be as throaty as possible. She must continually gargle, gurgle, mule, puke, croak, creak, hoop, and hawk, and if then she didn't bring down the house, well,—the fault was not hers.

Cassandra, who at any rate had a good memory, and did blindly what she was told to do, had just been through her part with faultless accuracy, and was a little hoarse after it, and no wonder. She had screamed, croaked, gurgled, gargled with pitiless precision, and on the last word she uttered, her voice, by an entirely unrehearsed effort, had cracked like a banjo string in a hot room. Mackay thought this particularly effective, and when he heard it was unpremeditated, urged her to practise it. He patted her on the back as she came off, and implied that if she acted like that in the performances, they would be very helpful to Æschylus's reputation. The other two stage directors, it is true, had intermittently indulged in unkind laughter during the performance, but Cassandra had not heard them, and if she had, she would not have cared.

At the end of the rehearsal the Babe stayed behind for a few moments to see about his dress, and passing across the stage again on his way out, found the three stage directors like the King, the Queen, and the Executioner in *Alice in Wonderland* in hot discussion. Like Alice, he was instantly appealed to by all three, and asked to give his opinion about Cassandra.

"Do you want me to say exactly what I think?" he asked.

"By all means," said Mackay, confidently.

The Babe hesitated a moment.

"I haven't criticised Cassandra at all," he said, "because I understood she was, so to speak, preserved. Also she is rather slow, and there would hardly be time for her to learn her part in the way I should suggest, and it would be a pity to confuse her mind farther. But if you ask what I think, she only reminds me of a strong young lady battling for reason against the clutches of delirium tremens."

The stage director who had seen so many French plays, smiled.

"I said drunk," he said.

"Drunk, certainly, and also I think beset by the black-beetle visions," said the Babe. "I daresay inspiration by Apollo may be like that, but I am afraid to an English audience it will suggest D. T."

"I thought she was splendid this morning," said Mackay.

"Well, I've told you what I think," said the Babe.

"What do you advise?"

"If there is time, I should advise her to remodel herself a little. Not to choke so much; she spits at me like a llama, you know. Not to be so inspired. There is too much saliva in her madness, I think."

"My dear fellow," broke in Mackay, "you miss the whole conception of the part. She is mad, stark, staring mad."

"I daresay I'm wrong," said the Babe.

There was an awkward pause, broken by Mackay who picked up his coat abruptly.

"Very well," said he. "Take her in hand yourselves. I must be going. We rehearse again at five, I think."

A moment's silence followed and they all looked at each other with the air of detected conspirators.

"Will you help us?" asked Dr. Propert at length of the Babe.

"Do you mean, will I coach Cassandra?"

"Yes."

The Babe hesitated.

"I don't want to interfere," he said, "but certainly there is room for improvement in Cassandra. And I don't want Mackay to think I am meddling with him. I would much sooner not."

"I think Mackay wishes it," said Propert, "only he didn't like saying so."

The Babe shrugged his shoulders.

"I didn't gather that from his manner, but if you can assure me of it, I will do my best with her."

Dr. Propert heaved a sigh of relief.

"Too many cooks spoil the broth," he said magnanimously. "We have too many stage directors. We all of us really want you to manage the whole thing. Some one will say your part this afternoon—I will myself—if you will take the rehearsal alone. Besides, the architecture of the palace is all wrong, and I have found a fifth century statue with sandals on. There is a cast of it in the Museum, and I must get it copied. We have our hands too full."

So that afternoon Dr. Propert read out Clytemnestra's part, and the two other stage directors sat meekly in corners, and busied themselves with sandals, and from the centre of the stalls the Babe issued his orders, while Dr. Propert read his part in a fine sonorous voice and in a modern Greek accent, which made the Iambic lines, so said Mackay, who had made a special study of ancient metres, sound like minor Galliambics. Cassandra exhibited mild surprise when the Babe stopped her gurgling, and when he forbade her to ogle the place where the Ophicleide should be, she felt like an unanchored ship, drifting helplessly about among quicksands. So the Babe reserved her for private instruction, and told Agamemnon not to go like Agag.

There was only a fortnight more before the performance, and the Babe worked like a horse, and like Hans Müller made miracles. The casual visitor to his rooms was likely to be confronted with a raging prophetess or a credulous king, in front of whom stood the Babe showing them how to rage or how to express the extremes of credulity. Dr. Propert found enough to do in superintending the stage properties and the second stage director became a sort of benignant elderly Mercury to the Babe. Mackay alone held slightly aloof.

On the night of the first performance, there was a thick, palpable atmosphere of nerves abroad, like a London fog. Agamemnon kept repeating his first line over and over again and wiping his hands on his himation, and tried to remember that, whatever he did, he must not clear his throat before he began to speak. The calm and prosy Argive elders put by their prosiness and became peppery; Dr. Propert flew about with altar wreaths in his hands, which he deposited carefully in safe places and then forgot where he had put them. Even the placid, moon-faced Cassandra pricked her fingers violently with her fifth-century brooch. As for the watchman it was a serious matter for doubt whether his shaking knees would ever take him safely down his somewhat ricketty watch-tower. The Babe alone, on whom really the whole responsibility as well as the heaviest part rested, towered head and shoulders above the nervous fog, and was absolutely his own silly self. He caught up Agamemnon three minutes before the curtain was to rise and tried to induce him to dance a *pas de quatre* out of the palace, and when Agamemnon trembled so that there was imminent risk of the sandals coming off, let alone dancing, danced a *pas seul* himself. He set Mr. Sykes upon the altar and crowned him with roses. He said he couldn't remember a word of his part, and proposed to act the execution of Mary Queen of Scots instead or send the audience empty away. He peeped through the spy-hole of the curtain and said the conductor hadn't come, which sent Dr. Propert flying round to see what had happened, whereas he had been in his place for ten minutes. In fact, he crowded, as he said, into five minutes of glorious life, the fatuities of years. The effect of all this was that the rest of the company were so completely taken up with deploring his behaviour, that they quite forgot to be nervous, which was precisely the end which the Babe had in view.

The performance rose to the level of excellence, and Cassandra maintained it, but Clytemnestra——the pens of the critics failed before Clytemnestra. They couldn't, they confessed, do her justice. She was a creation, a revelation, an incarnation; she was wonderful, marvellous, stupendous, gorgeous, inimitable, irresistible, unapproachable, inexplicable. She held the mirror up to Nature, the κάτοπτρον up to art, and the *speculum* up to drama—this was a little involved, and Dr. Propert is responsible. A shaggy student from Heidelberg who represented his university, thought she was a woman, and, heedless of Agamemnon's doom, fell in love with her on the spot, and was disposed to take it as a personal insult that the Babe was of the sex that Nature made him. However, as marriage was out of the question, he wrote an appreciative article in the Heidelberg *Mittheilungen* on Clytemnestrismos (made in Germany), contrasting it with Agamemnonismos, with a great deal about the standpoint of the subjective Ego, in the presence of objective archaism. She held the house, she entranced the audience, she dominated their imaginations; she tore away the veil of realism from in front of idealism (whatever that may mean); she gilded Æschylus's conception, and enriched his execution. She was Clytemnestra. And then they began all over again with variations.

Every night at the fall of the curtain, the Babe was called back again and again, every night the whole house rose at him like one man, and the florist outside the theatre must have realised a competence for the rest of his days. It had been a rather dull and uneventful term, the University wanted something to go mad about, and stark staring mad it went. If Cambridge had not been in a Christian country, it would have had a Babe-cult on the spot. His photograph, taken at the great moment when he came out with "murder beaming from every line of his countenance" as the *Cambridge Daily News* finely observed, and slowly wrung his hands free of the blood that dripped from them, was in half the shops in the town. For the second time—a unique distinction—he was in authority in the "Granta," and the *Cambridge Review* had a long article entirely about him, beginning, "It must surely have occurred to any thoughtful critic." Night after night the cry of "Speech"—what could have been less appropriate than that Clytemnestra should make an English speech after a Greek play?—went up from a crowded house, and as regularly the Babe bowed and smiled and shook his black-wigged head, and gracefully declined. Once—it was most indecorous and improper—he went so far as to whistle to Sykes who was always in attendance, and made him bark, but otherwise the attempt to get a speech from the Babe was as unprofitable as trying to get water out of a stone. And his performance was the more remarkable in that he did not repeat himself slavishly: acting was an instinct with him, and each night he acted as his mood prompted him. For instance, his manner of entry after the murder, changed every night. Once he stood at the palace door quite silent for nearly a couple of minutes, until Dr. Propert turned quite pale with the thought that perhaps the prompter might think that he wanted prompting, and spoil the moment, wiping his hands slowly, and smiling a ghastly smile at the chorus; once he came out quickly and threw the axe away from him and plunged into his speech; once, and an audible horror ran round the house as he did it, he broke into the silence by a mirthless laugh as he fondled the axe with which he had done the deed, like a mother nursing her child. In a word, he made it clear, that Æschylus was a most excellent dramatist, and that he was a most excellent actor.

XVI
After Lunch

I shall be by the fire, suppose.
Browning.

There were only three weeks more to the end of the term, but as soon as the play was over, the Babe at once settled down again to his social and historical duties. With December a hard frost had set in, and football for a time was at a standstill. But next to football as an after lunch amusement, the Babe preferred above everything else a warm room, a large chair, and congenial company. With these objects in view he asked Reggie and Ealing to lunch with him one day, and entirely refused to go out afterwards. Reggie, who had a sort of traditional notion that people always went out after lunch, or else they were ill, was overruled by the Babe, who sent his gyp out to order muffins for tea, and drew his chair close up to the fire.

"But it's such a jolly day, Babe," said Reggie, who was only half persuaded.

The Babe looked out of the window and shuddered.

"By that you mean that there is a horrid smell of frost in the air, that the sun looks like a copper plate, and that by walking very fast and putting on woollen gloves you can get completely warm, with the exception of the end of your nose. I hate woollen gloves, I hate walking fast, and I hate the tip of my nose to be cold. I avoid all these things by sitting by the fire."

"Fuggy brute."

"About my being a brute," said the Babe, "there may be two opinions. But fuggy, as you call it, I am. I confess it, and I glory in it. At the same time I'm no fuggier than you. If you had your way you would go a nasty walk in order to get fuggy. We both want to be fuggy, and I merely adopt the easiest method of becoming so. Dear Reggie, you are so very English. You love taking the greatest possible trouble to secure your object. That is called the Sporting Instinct. Personally I am not troubled with a sluggish liver, but if I was I should take a pill. That would not suit English people at all: instead of taking a pill, they take exercise, purely medicinally, and they always adopt the most circuitous ways of taking it. What can be a more elaborate method of guarding against a sluggish liver than spending three thousand pounds on building a tennis court, which can only be used by two people at a time?"

"What do you play Rugger for, then?"

"Why, because it is the most expeditious way possible of getting exercise. You concentrate into an hour the exercise you couldn't get under half a day if you went a walk."

"I have known you get keen about it," said Reggie. "Was that only because you admired the expedition with which you were getting exercise?"

The Babe yawned.

"We'll change the subject," he said. "I've been asked to your Comby on the 6th. I don't know why a college should celebrate the birthday of their founder by making scurrilous rhymes about each other, but I'm quite glad that they should, and I have very kindly consented to come."

"Thanks, awfully," said Ealing.

"Don't mention it. But really it's a very interesting point, as Longridge would say. You all go to chapel, and they sing 'Zadok the priest.' Then you have a big feed in Hall, and the whole college assembles together, and they libel each other in decasyllable couplets. Luckily there's no rhyme to Babe."

"There are heaps," said Reggie precipitously.

"I think none. Talking of Longridge, he is supposed to be perfecting a plan by which, as you walk up to your door you tread on a spring, and the door flies open. He says it is so tiresome to open a door when your hands are full. And his hands always are full."

"It sounds very pleasant," said Reggie. "Has he tried it yet?"

"Only once. That time his door was already open, and when he trod on the spring, it shut with, I believe, quite incredible violence and knocked all his books out of his hands, besides hurting him very much and breaking his spectacles. You'd think that would stop him? Not a bit. He merely rose on the stepping-stone of his dead self to higher things. It only gave him another new idea. He is going to have a second spring inside the door, which, when trodden on will shut it again after you. At least that's what he means to do, when he is fit to walk about again. At present he is incapacitated. I went to see him yesterday; his nose is in splints. I am so glad I haven't an ingenious mind."

"I wouldn't be Longridge's bed-maker, if I was paid for it."

"Bed-makers are paid for it," said the Babe. "Besides, as he truly says, if you can have a dumb waiter why not have a dumb bed-maker made of some stronger material?"

"He never said anything of the kind, Babe," said Ealing.

"My dear chap, he has said lots of things of the kind. You force me to contradict you. He hardly ever says anything of any other kind."

"Babe, will you or will you not come out?" demanded Reggie.

"I will not come out. I'm not going to spoil my tea by going for a horrid walk."

"I wish you would listen to reason."

The Babe murmured something inaudible about there being no reason to listen, but when pressed, confessed that he had been reading the *Green Carnation* and it had affected his brains.

But Reggie, following, as the Babe said, "that blind instinct which makes us Englishmen what we are"—he was taking liberties with the remarks made by his fellow-guest at the T.A.F.—insisted on going out and taking Ealing with him, though promising to come back for tea, and the Babe was left to himself.

He was conscious of feeling a little flat, now that the Greek play was over, and he half wondered to himself what he had done before it began, to get through the time. For instance, to-day it was barely half-past three, he was not going to dine till eight, and he had already done as much work as he meant to do. He thought bitterly that Dr. Watts had very much overrated Satan's powers of invention. The upshot was that he fell asleep and Reggie and Ealing returning an hour later found him stewing contentedly in front of the fire.

The Babe was rather cross at being awakened, and he said they smelt horribly frosty. Also he wished the door to be shut, and he was very hungry. Why were they so unkind, and what had he done to deserve this? But the muffins came before long, and the Babe recovered his admirable serenity under the cheering influence of most of them.

"And though your muffin," he remarked, "is said to destroy the coats of the stomach, no such ill effects will be experienced if the patient takes enough of them. My only misgiving is that I have not taken enough. And yet I have taken all."

"How much dinner do you suppose you will be able to eat?" asked Reggie, who was still gazing incredulously at the empty dish which the Babe had put on the table close to him.

"As much as Stewart will be kind enough to give me. And his board is usually plentifully spread. If he asks me to dinner much oftener I shall feel bound in common gratitude to tell him the truth about my royal visitor in the Long. I wish I'd had a photograph of the group taken, Jack really looked too splendid."

"Jack has the makings of a comedian about him," said Reggie, "but just now he's very serious. There is an epidemic of sapping abroad, but if it wasn't sapping, it would probably be influenza, so we can't complain. You're touched with it, Babe, and Jack's got it badly. I went to see him yesterday, and he was analysing the second Punic war in a large square note-book with notes on the Wasps at the other end."

"I know. And he was quite angry when I ventured to speak disrespectfully of Hannibal. He called me a funny ass, and implied that Hannibal was more than a father to him. Also he has taken to red ink which is one of the worst signs. I went into his room in the dark one day last week, and upset something. It proved to be a stone bottle of red ink, rather larger than a ginger-beer bottle and quite full. Also the cork was out, and after that there was no further need for the cork. It would have been like locking the stable door when the steed was spilt—I mean, stolen. I pointed that out to him, for it was surely consoling to know that no more red ink could be spilt in his rooms, unless he was rash enough to buy some more, in which case, so to speak, it would have been on his own head, which would be worse than on the carpet, but he only murmured, 'Caius Flaminius Secundus,' and asked if I was sitting on his classical dictionary."

"And were you?"

"I think it turned out that he was. So I called him a sap, and went away."

"I hate a sap," said Reggie with a certain dignity.

"We used to call a sap a groutbags at my private school," said Ealing.

"Why?"

"I don't know what else you could call them. I was a groutbags once myself."

The Babe yawned.

"I feel rather futile," he said. "I wanted to be amused, and you fellows would go for a walk. Let's play 'Kiss in the slipper,' or something."

"I hear you played Van John till two this morning," said Reggie.

The Babe stopped in the middle of his yawn.

"Yes, a little after two, I think. We played Van John and other things. I lost six pounds. Blow the expense. Do you know Feltham of this college?"

"No, why?"

"Oh, nothing. He was there, that's all."

"Nice chap?"

"Nothing particular. Oh, yes, quite nice, I should think, but he went away as soon as we shut up playing. I hardly know him—in fact I never met him before. Hullo, it's seven. I must go."

"Where are you going?"

"Only to see a man I know, as the Apostles say. Are either of you dining with Stewart to-night?"

"Yes, I am," said Reggie. "At eight, isn't it?"

"Yes. Be punctual, because I'm so hungry."

XVII
A Little Game

Whist is slow, but baccarat bites,
Baccarat bites, and we want to be bit;
Late comes dawn on these winter nights,
And you need no knowledge to play at it.
Hotch-potch Verses.

In all his life for two years and a half at Cambridge, and he had associated with very many classes there, the Babe had never come across any man whom he would suspect of being capable of doing that which necessitated his going to see "the man" he knew on such an errand as this, and he concluded rightly that though such people no doubt occurred, they were not to be looked for, with any chance of finding them, at university towns. His errand was not a pleasant one, and it was far from being an easy one, and when he knocked at Feltham's door a few minutes afterwards, he could not have hazarded the vaguest guess as to what manner of exit he would make.

The Babe was, unfortunately, strongly possessed by the gambling instinct, and when the night before a friend of his had come in after Hall, and proposed whist if they could get a four, the Babe said that if they were going to play cards, they might as well play something more amusing than whist, which seemed to him as a peculiarly unexhilarating mode of enjoying oneself, and which he regarded as a practical application of unmixed mathematics. If Broxton would raise two people to play at something more biting than whist, the Babe would raise two others.

The Babe raised his two without much delay, but Broxton returned with only one. However, he said he had met a chap called Feltham, who, he knew, played, and should he see whether he could come?

The Babe would have played cards with old Gooseberry himself, if he could not get anyone else, so Broxton went off to see whether Feltham would play, found him in and willing, and they played Van John for a while, until the Babe began to yawn and complained he had only lost three and six.

Did they know Marmara, which was indifferently called "Only-a-penny," chiefly because it dealt with sums usually much larger than that.

Some of them, and among these was Feltham, did know Marmara, and the others were willing to learn it. So the Babe, assuring them that no previous knowledge was required, proceeded to enlighten them. Everyone placed a small sum, say sixpence, or its equivalent in counters, in the pool, and the dealer thereupon dealt three cards face downwards all around, and three to himself. He then turned up the next card, and you had all your premises.

Thus—if, for instance, the card turned up happened to be a four of diamonds, each player in turn had to bet, before looking at his three cards which lay face downwards on the table, whether they contained a diamond higher than the four. His stake was only limited by the sum in the pool unless they chose to fix a smaller limit. Thus with the four turned up, it would probably appear to each player that there was a fair chance of his holding a higher card of the same suit, and he would in all likelihood stake pretty well as high as he could. He would then turn up his cards, and if his hand held a diamond higher than the four, he would have the pleasure of taking the amount of his stake out of the pool, if not, the pain of paying into the pool the same sum.

The game, so said the Babe, was amusing, owing to the fact that it was pure hazard, and also because the pool mounted up in a way that would seem to the uninitiated simply incredible. An example of this occurred at the fifth deal. At the beginning of this deal the pool contained four shillings. The Babe dealt, and turned up the two of spades. The first player naturally enough went the pool, but his hand very curiously contained only diamonds, and he paid four shillings into the pool, thus raising it to eight. Even more naturally, since the first player had held no spades, the second player again staked the pool. His hand contained two hearts and a club, and the pool became sixteen shillings. It would have been midsummer madness in the third player, who was Broxton, not to stake the pool, and as it was November and he was perfectly sane, he did so. His hand revealed three splendid hearts, and the pool rose to thirty-two shillings. The chances were thus enormously in favour of the fourth player clearing the pool, and he accordingly staked it. But as he held a diamond and two clubs, he paid the pool the equivalent of thirty-two shillings, in mean bone counters, belonging to the Babe. There was nothing left for the fifth player, who was Feltham, to do but to stake the pool, which he did. His hand, oddly enough, contained the seven, eight, and nine of clubs, and he remarked quite unreasonably, as he paid sixty-four shillings into the pool, that the cards had not been shuffled. Thus the Babe, who had dealt, had a pool of sixty-four shillings to win or lose. He staked the pool, but he held one diamond, one club, and the ace of spades, which counted below the two, and he wrote an I O U for sixty-four shillings, as he had not got enough counters, and paid it into the pool, remarking that this was better than whist at three penny points. Then the pool in one deal had mounted from four shillings, to one hundred and twenty-eight shillings, and it was obvious that if a similar deal occurred again now, there would be a very considerable sum in the pool at the end of it.

The Babe in these matters was, like the Athenians, somewhat superstitious, and he said cheerfully that it was a mounting pool, and they would have some amusement. The pool showed by its subsequent conduct that he was right, and at the end of an hour it held about £50, about half of which had been contributed by Feltham, whose luck had been abominable. This, as they were playing at present, might be won by anybody, since there was no limit to the stakes, and the Babe, with the best possible motives, since he was the only one present who would not be somewhat embarrassed by the total loss of his contribution to the pool, proposed setting a limit, of, say, twenty-five shillings to the stake. Feltham objected strongly, and the alteration was vetoed.

Everyone, with the exception perhaps of the Babe, was a little excited and on edge, for when two or three are gathered together to gamble they often generate spontaneously between them—this is a sober fact—a little demon which hovers about and unsettles their nerves. Feltham especially hardly spoke, except to name his stake, and sometimes to swear when he lost it, and the Babe felt that they were all taking it too seriously and quite spoiling his pleasure. For himself, he liked a "little game" because it happened to amuse him, but the others were behaving as if they cared whether they won money or lost money, and this, to the Babe's thinking, spoilt the whole thing. The point of gambling, according to him, was not whether you won money or lost money, but the moment when it was uncertain whether you were going to win (in the abstract) or lose (in the abstract). The view is wholly unreasonable, and so is the gambling instinct.

It was Broxton's turn to deal. He dealt badly, holding the pack from which he dealt nearly a foot above the table, so that if any of them happened to be looking at the cards as they were dealt to him, the chances were that he would get a glimpse or a hint of what the under one was, and once before that evening the Babe had demanded a fresh deal, because as his cards were dealt him, he could not help seeing the corner of a picture card. This time, however, he was handing a cigarette to Feltham, who sat on his right. But as Feltham's cards were dealt him the Babe saw him look up quickly, and he himself saw the face of one of them, so far, at least, that he would have been ready to swear it was a picture card in clubs. Feltham at the moment seemed to him to open his mouth to speak, but said nothing and only glanced hurriedly at the Babe, who did not look at him again during the game. The turn-up card was the nine of clubs.

The first two players naturally enough, as there were only four cards out of fifty-two which could beat the nine, staked a nominal stake merely, and turned up their cards. One of them held the king of clubs, and this would have won, leaving only three cards in the pack which could win. He took a shilling, the amount of his stake, out of the pool, and said he wished he had trusted to his instinct. It was Feltham's turn. He staked £20, which was madness. His hand contained the queen of clubs and he won.

Very soon after, the Babe renewed his proposition that they should limit the stakes, and this time there was no opposition, and as it was already after one, they settled to stop as soon as the pool had been emptied. The pool, seeing them change their tactics, also changed its own, and instead of mounting continued to sink steadily. Every now and then it would go up again by a couple of limit stakes, but the constant tendency was to sink, and in three-quarters of an hour it was empty. Broxton gathered up the cards and counters, and Feltham and two of the others said "Good-night," and left the room, but Anstruther and the Babe sat down and waited. The Babe helped himself to whisky, tore up his own I O U's which he had paid for, and there was a long awkward silence.

Broxton got up, closed the door, and came and stood in front of the fire.

"That fellow cheated," he said at last. "I saw him, twice. Did you notice, Babe?"

"I thought he saw the cards which were dealt him once. The turn-up was a nine of clubs and he staked £20. It struck me as unusual, particularly as the king was already out."

"Then he cheated twice, as Jim said," answered Anstruther. "I am convinced he saw his cards once before, both times when Jim was dealing."

"Jim, you damned fool," said the Babe, "why can't you manage to deal properly?"

"We're all damned fools, I think," said Broxton. "What business have we got to ask a fellow to play whom we don't know, and who probably can't afford it."

"Nor can I," said Anstruther, "but I don't cheat."

"Are we quite sure he did cheat?" asked the Babe.

"Personally, I am," said Broxton, "aren't you, Anstruther?"

"Good Lord, yes."

"Well, what's to be done?" asked the Babe.

"The men who play with him ought to know," said Anstruther.

The Babe got up, and threw his torn-up I O U's into the fire.

"Rot," he said. "We can't possibly be certain. And I'm not going to ask him to play again in order to watch him. That seems to me perhaps one degree lower than cheating oneself. It's our own fault, as Jim said, for asking him."

"My dear Babe, we can't leave it as it is."

"No, I don't want to do that. I only meant that we couldn't tell other people what we suspected, unless we were certain, and not even then. And we can't be certain unless we play with him again, and that I don't mean to do."

"What *do* you propose to do then?"

"I propose that one of us tells him what we thought we saw."

"And if he denies it?"

"The matter ends there. At the same time to make it clear to him that three people separately thought they saw him."

"Thought they saw him!" said Broxton.

"Certainly. Thought they saw him. I daresay he isn't a bad chap. I daresay he was playing for far more than he could afford. It is even possible he will confess he did cheat, and it is quite possible that we are all wrong and that he didn't. Personally I certainly thought he did, but I wouldn't take my oath on it."

"Who's to ask him?"

There was a short silence. Then—

"I will, if you like," said the Babe.

"Thanks, Babe," said Jim, "you'd do it better than either of us."

The Babe lit a cigarette, and finished his whisky.

"I'm off to bed," he said, "I would sooner have played 'old maid' than that this should have happened. Of course none of us say a word about it? Good-night, you chaps."

Anstruther and Broxton sat on for a bit after the Babe had gone.

"It's a devilish business," said the latter at length. "But I'm sure the Babe will manage it as well as it can be managed."

"The Babe isn't half a bad chap," said Anstruther.

"No, I don't think he is. In fact, I don't think I ever knew a better. Are you off? Good-night."

The Babe wrote a note to Feltham next morning asking him if he would be in at seven that evening, and receiving an affirmative answer, it thus came about that he tapped at his door at that hour.

XVIII
The Confession

Qui s'accuse, s'excuse.
From the French.

The Babe's supposition that Feltham "perhaps wasn't a bad chap" was perfectly correct. At the same time it is perfectly true that he had cheated at cards, which, quite rightly, is one of the few social crimes for which a man is ostracised.

He had cheated, and he knew it, and he was thoroughly, honestly, and unreservedly ashamed of it. He did not try to console himself by the fact that he had never done it before, and by the knowledge that he would never do it again, because he knew that he would fail to find the slightest consolation in that, though it was perfectly true. The thing was done and it was past mending. Twice he had seen the cards, or at any rate had a suspicion of one of them, when they were dealt him, without saying anything. On one of these occasions what he had seen did not help him, for he saw only a card of another suit, but once, when he had seen the queen of clubs, he traded on it, and swindled the company of £20.

How he had come to do it, he did not know. He thought the devil must have taken possession of him, and he was probably quite right. The temptation was the stronger because he had lost, as the Babe had suggested, much more than he could afford, and the thing was done almost before he meant to do it. He more than half suspected that the Babe had noticed it, but to do him justice this suspicion weighed very light in his mind, compared with the fact that he had cheated.

Next morning the Babe's note came, and his suspicion that the Babe had noticed it took definite form. It was no manner of use refusing to see him, but what he could not make up his mind about, was what answer he should give him. To confess it would not help him to make reparation, and to return, as he honestly wanted to do, the £20 he had won and besides it did not seem, in anticipation, particularly an easy thing to do. And when the Babe knocked at his door, he was still as much in the dark as ever, as to what, if the Babe's errand was what he suspected, he should say to him.

The Babe accepted a cigarette, and sat down rather elaborately. He had determined not to remark upon the weather or the prospects of an early dissolution, or make any foolish attempts to lead up to the subject, and after a moment he spoke.

"I am awfully sorry," he said, "to have to say what I am going to. In two words it is this: Three men with whom you were playing last night at Marmara, thought that once or twice you saw your cards, or one of your cards, before you staked. I am one of them myself, and we decided that the only fair and proper thing to do was to ask you whether this was so. I am very sorry to have to say this."

The Babe behaved like the gentleman he was, and instead of looking at Feltham to see whether his face indicated anything, kept his eyes steadily away from him.

Feltham stood a moment without answering and if the Babe had chosen to look at him he would have seen that he paused because he could not command his voice. But the Babe did not choose to do so. Feltham would have given anything that moment to have been able to say "It is true," but it seemed to him a physical impossibility. On the other hand he felt it equally impossible to take the high line, to threaten to kick the Babe out of the room unless he went in double quick time etc., etc.,—to do any of those things which thorough-paced swindlers are supposed to do when their honour is quite properly called in question.

"It is a damned lie," he said at length, quite quietly and without conviction.

The Babe got up at once, and stepped across to where Feltham was standing.

"Then I wish to apologise most sincerely both for myself and the other two fellows," he said, "and if you would like to knock me down, you may. I shall of course tell them at once we were mistaken, and I believe what you say entirely. Will you shake hands?"

Feltham let the Babe take his hand, and as the latter turned to leave the room, sat limply down in the chair from which the Babe had got up.

But the Babe had hardly got half-way across the room, when Feltham spoke again.

The Babe's utter frankness had suddenly made it impossible for Feltham to let him go without telling him, but to tell him now was not made easier by having lied about it.

"Please wait a minute," he said.

The Babe's cigarette had gone out, and he lit it again over the lamp. Then he sat down in the window seat and waited. Outside, the grass was sparkling with frost and the clock chimed a quarter past seven. Simultaneously Feltham spoke:

"I have lied to you as well," he said. "What you saw was perfectly true. I cheated twice, at least I saw one of the cards dealt me twice, and said nothing about it. Once the card happened to be immaterial, and once I staked £20 knowing I should win. I have told you all."

The Babe was a person of infinite variety, and if those who knew him best had seen him now, they would hardly have believed it was he. He sat down on the arm of the chair where Feltham was sitting, and to himself cursed the whole pack of cards from ace to king, and above all Jim Broxton. Then aloud—

"My poor dear fellow," he said. "I'm devilish sorry for you."

Feltham, who had been expecting to hear a few biting remarks or else merely the door slam behind the Babe, looked up. The Babe was looking at him, quite kindly, quite naturally, as if he was condoling with him on some misfortune.

Feltham began, "Damn it all—" then stopped, and without a moment's warning burst out crying.

The Babe got up, went to the door and sported it. Then he sat down again on the arm of the chair.

"Poor chap," he said. "It's beastly hard lines, and I fully expect it's as much our fault as yours. You needn't trouble to tell me you never did it before: of course you didn't. I fully believe that. People who would confess that sort of thing don't do that sort of thing twice. It was like this perhaps— we were playing for far more than you could afford, and you didn't mean to do it, until somehow it was done. Money is a devilish contrivance."

"Yes, it was just like that," said Feltham. "As I told you, the first time I saw a card, it didn't make any difference, though of course I ought to have said so. But the second time it did, and before I knew what I had done, I had cheated. Why don't you call me a swindler and tell me I'm not fit to associate with gentlemen? It's God's truth."

The corners of the Babe's mouth twitched.

"It's not my concern then. What would be the good of saying that?"

He paused a moment, hoping that Feltham would make a certain suggestion, and he was not disappointed.

"Look here, there's the twenty pounds: what can I do with it? Can you help me?"

The Babe thought a moment.

"Yes, give it me. I'll see that the other fellows get it somehow, if you'll leave it to my discretion. And, you know, it sounds absurd for a fool like me to give advice, but if I were you I shouldn't play cards for money again. It's no use running one's head into danger. If it's not rude, what is your allowance?"

"Two hundred and fifty."

"You bally ass! Yet I don't know. It's our fault. You couldn't tell that the pool would behave in that manner, and I know, personally, I should find it out of the question to say one was playing for more than one could afford. Some people call it moral cowardice, it seems to me a perfectly natural reticence."

"Of course I won't play again," said Feltham. "Why have you been so awfully good to me?"

"I haven't. What else was I to do? Oh, yes, and I think I respected you for telling the truth. Most fellows would have lied like George Washington."

Feltham smiled feebly.

"All that remains is this," said the Babe. "Of course I must tell those other two fellows about it, the two I mean with whom I talked, but you can trust them absolutely. It is impossible that anyone else should ever know about it."

"You don't think—oughtn't I to tell them all?" stammered Feltham.

The Babe frowned.

"Of course you ought not. Why the deuce should you? About the money—it must be divided up between us all. Six into twenty, about three pound ten each. Rather an awkward sum."

"Why six?"

"Because there were six of us."

"I can't take any."

"Your feelings have nothing to do with it," remarked the Babe. "The money in the pool of course belongs to everyone. You return the others' shares of that £20 and keep your own. Well, I'll manage it somehow. I will make absurd bets, seventy to one in shillings. That will surprise nobody: I often do it. Good Lord, it's a quarter to eight. If you're going into Hall, you'll be very late, and so shall I for my dinner. I must go. Oh, by the way, did you lose much altogether?"

"About twenty-five pounds."

"Is it, is it"—began the Babe. "I mean, are you in a hole? If so, I wish you'd let me lend you some money. Why shouldn't you? No? Are you sure you don't want some? It's no use receiving unpleasant letters from one's father, when there's no need. Well as you like. Good-night. Come round and look me up some time: I'm on the next stair-case."

Feltham followed him to the door.

"I can't tell you what I feel," he said huskily, "but I am not ungrateful. Half an hour ago you asked me to shake hands with you. Will you shake hands with me?"

"Why, surely," said the Babe.

XIX
In the Fifties

He sailed his little paper boats,
And when the folk thought scorn of that,
He spudded up the waiting worm
And yearned towards the master's hat.
Hotch-potch Verses.

The Babe went off to dress for dinner much relieved in mind. Now that it was over he confessed to himself that he had been quite certain that Feltham had cheated, but that he should own up to it, was fine, and the Babe who considered himself totally devoid of anything which could possibly be construed into moral courage, respected him for it. He also registered a vow that never to the crack of doom—which cracked three days afterwards—would he play unlimited Marmara again, and told himself that he was not cut out for the sort of thing that he had just been through, and that he was glad it was over. He went round at once to tell Broxton and Anstruther what had happened, and after that shook the whole

affair from his mind, as a puppy shakes itself after being in the water.

He was, naturally, late for dinner, and Mr. Stewart who knew the value of soup and also the habits of the Babe, had not waited. When he did appear, he was, of course, perfectly unabashed, and took the bottom of the table with unassuming grace.

"The psychology of punctuality," he remarked, "is a most interesting study. Some day I mean to study it, and I shall write a little monograph on the subject uniform with those which Sherlock Holmes wrote on tobacco ash and the tails of cart horses. I think there must be a punctuality bacillus, something like a death-watch, always ticking, and if there isn't one, I shall invent it. It doesn't take to me. I am too healthy."

"My dear Babe," said the Stewart, "you have disappointed me. I always hoped that you were the one person I have been looking for so long, who has never been punctual; But you have been punctual to my knowledge twice, once on an occasion in the Long——"

"When was that?" interrupted the Babe. "I don't believe it."

"On a memorable occasion. At lunch in your own rooms."

The Babe caught Reggie's eye, and looked away.

"Oh, yes."

"And as Clytemnestra, you always killed Agamemnon with ruthless punctuality. I was always hoping to hear him scream during the next Chorus but one."

"I did the screaming for him," said the Babe complacently, "except on the first night. He could only scream like an empty syphon."

"There is nothing more tragic or blood-curdling than the scream of an empty syphon," said Stewart. "It shrieks to you, like a banshee of all the whisky and soda you have drunk. The only thing that could shriek worse would be an empty whisky bottle, and that can't shriek at all. If he really could scream like that, you robbed him of a chance of greatness by screaming for him, although you screamed very well."

"There are syphons and syphons," said the Babe, "he screamed like an empty but undervitalised one, which had never really been full."

"Babe, if you talk about undervitalised syphons during fish," said Reggie, "you will drive us all mad, before the end of dinner."

"Going mad," said Mr. Stewart, "is an effort of will. I could go mad in a minute if I wished, and the Babe certainly determined to go mad when he was yet a boy. No offence meant, Babe. I can confidently state that during the three years I have known him, he has never for a moment seemed to be really sane."

"I was perfectly sane when I settled to go in for the tripos," said the Babe.

"You never settled to do anything of the kind. You think you did and it is one of your wildest delusions."

"Secondly I was sane," said the Babe, "when I—"

"No you weren't," put in Reggie.

"Reggie, don't be like Longridge. But you are quite right. I wasn't sane then, though I thought I was for the moment."

"Longridge is better, though he still has a large piece of sticking plaster over his nose," said Mr. Stewart. "He came to see me to-day. He insisted on arguing with me in spite of my expostulations. When he talks, I always want to cover him up, as one covers up a chirping canary."

"I wish you would do it some day. With a piece of green baize you know, and a hole in it where the handle of the cage comes out."

"He would continue to make confused noises within," said Reggie.

"He always makes confused noises," said Mr. Stewart wearily. "Confused, ingenious, noises. Babe, tell me if that champagne is drinkable."

The Babe drank off his glass.

"Obviously," he said. "But it's no use asking me: all champagne seems to me delicious. I drink Miller's cheapest for choice."

A small withered don who was sitting next the Babe, and had not previously spoken, here looked up.

"A nice, dry, light wine," he said.

The Babe started violently, and if he had not just emptied his glass of champagne, he would certainly have spilled it. He explained afterwards that he really had forgotten that anyone was occupying the chair on the right.

This curious old gentlemen, one of the few surviving specimens of this particular type of elderly don had the classical name of Moffat, and Mr. Stewart at once introduced him to the Babe, a ceremony which had escaped his memory before, and Mr. Moffat who had been shivering on the brink of conversation all dinner, decided to plunge in.

"I saw your performance of the *Agamemnon* last week," he said.

"I hope you enjoyed it," said the Babe politely.

"The stage is not what it was in me young days," said Mr. Moffat.

The Babe looked interested and waited for further criticisms, but the old gentleman returned to his dinner without offering any. His face looked as if it was made of cast iron, painted with Aspinall's buff-coloured enamel.

There was a short silence, and Mr. Stewart, looking up, saw that the Babe was fighting like a man against an inward convulsion of laughter. His face changed from pink to red, and a vein stood out on his usually unwrinkled brow. Stewart knew that when the Babe had a fit of the giggles it was, so to speak, no laughing matter, and he made things worse by asking Mr. Moffat how his sister was. At this point the Babe left the room with a rapid, uneven step, and he was heard to plunge violently into the dishes outside. Stewart had been particularly unfortunate in his choice of a subject, because what had started the Babe off, was the very thought that Mr. Moffat's sister was no doubt the original Miss Moffat, and he had been rashly indulging in wild conjectures as to what would happen if he said suddenly:

"I believe your sister doesn't like spiders."

Mr. Moffat had resumed the subject of the Greek play when the Babe returned—he seemed not to have noticed his ill-mannered exit—and was finding fault with the chorus, particularly with the leader, who, in the person of Reggie, was sitting opposite him. Of this, however, he had not the slightest idea.

"I call them a dowdy crew," he said. "They were dressed like old baize doors. Not me idea of a chorus at all. But it was all very creditable, very creditable indeed, and we have to thank me young friend here for a very fine performance of Clytemnestra. Why, me sister"—here the Babe gasped for a moment like a drowning man, but recovered himself bravely—"me sister came down next morning at breakfast, and said she'd hardly been able to sleep a wink, hardly a wink, for thinking of Clytemnestra."

The Babe made a violent effort and checked himself.

"I'm so sorry," he said, with his most engaging manner. "I hope you will apologise to her for me."

"Not at all, not at all," said Mr. Moffat. "It's me own opinion she slept far more than she knew. But she was always nervous,"—the Babe bit his tongue—"easily upset. A very good pheasant, Mr. Stewart, a very good pheasant. Thank ye, yes, a glass of champagne. A glass of wine with you, heh, heh, Clytemnestra."

Mr. Moffat, as the Babe allowed afterwards, was a very pleasant old gentleman. When dinner was over and he had settled himself into an arm-chair by the fire, smoking one of Stewart's strongest cigars, he told several stories about the old generation of dons whom he had known.

"There was an old fellow of King's" he was saying, "in me undergraduate days, who must have been eighty, and never a night had he spent out of Cambridge since he came up as an undergraduate. An infidel old lot he was. Many a time I've seen him in the evening, when the worms were come out on the grass plot, hobbling about and trying to kill them with the point of his stick. He used to talk to them and make faces at them and say, 'Ah, damn you. You haven't got me yet.' A queer lot they all were, not the worms I mean, heh, heh, but the old dons. There were two others who had been great mathematicians in their time, and they used to spend their evenings together doing, what do you think? Making paper boats, sir, which they went and sailed on the Cam next day. They would start them from the King's bridge, and sail them down to the willow at the other end of the lawn. And such quarrels as they had over which had won! One of them one morning, his name was Jenkinson, if I'm not mistaken, an old Yorkshireman, got so heated over it,—for he said the other boat had fouled his, as if they were racing for a cup,—that he went for the other man, by gad, sir, he went for him, and tried to push him into the river. But the other—his name was Keggs—was too quick for him, and stepped out of the way, and head over ears into the river went Jenkinson himself, being unable to stop himself, sir, by reason of the impetus he had got up. The river isn't over deep, there, as you know, perhaps two feet deep, and he stood up as soon as he could find his feet and bawled out: 'Ah misdoot ye've drooned me, Keggs.'"

The Babe was delighted.

"Do tell me some more," he said, when Mr. Moffat had finished laughing himself, which he did in a silent, internal manner.

"Ah, some of those old fellows did things not quite fit for boys to hear about. *Maxima reverentia*, eh, Mr. Stewart? But there was an Irishman, a fellow of Clare too, in my time. I might tell you about him; he used to live in the rooms above the gate. He had a quarrel with the Master, and as often as the Master went in and out of the gate, egad, the old chap would try to spit on his head. If the Master was out to dinner, he would wait up, sitting in his window till he came back, be it eleven o'clock or twelve, or later than that. At last the Master had to put up an umbrella when he walked under the gate of his own college and then the old fellow would shout out, 'Come, out o' that, ye ould divil, and let me get at ye.' A disreputable old crew they were!—Ah well, it's half-past ten. Eleven's me bedtime, and I must be going. Good-night to you Mr. Stewart, and many thanks for your kind hospitality. And good-night to you, sir," he said turning to the Babe; "I heard them shout 'Clytemnestra, good old Clytemnestra,' after you all down the street. And you deserved an ovation, sir, you richly deserved an ovation, and I'm glad you got it."

After Mr. Moffat's departure, they settled down again, and Stewart remarked:

"You've made a conquest, Babe. But you behaved abominably during dinner."

"I couldn't help it. I could think of nothing but Miss Moffat. On the top of that you enquired about his sister. I ask you, what was I to do?"

"You needn't have danced in the dishes outside," said Reggie.

"I only danced in the soup, and we'd finished with the soup. And there's a soupçon of it on my—"

"Shut up."

"Pumps," continued the Babe. "May I have some whisky? Thanks. For what I'm going to receive. What a funny undergraduate Moffat must have been."

"I believe he was born like that," said Stewart. "I know when I came up, ten years ago, he was just the same. That's the best of getting old early: you don't change any more."

"That's one for you, Babe," remarked Reggie.

"The Babe is the imperishable child," said Stewart.

"You called me a man of the world the other day," said the Babe in self-defence.

"I think not."

"You did really. However, we'll pass it over."

"By the way, Babe, you are corrupting the youth of the college. Two men went into their lodgings last night at ten minutes past two. It transpired that they had been playing cards with you."

"Well, it is true that I was playing cards last night. But they could have gone away earlier if they had wished."

"Your fascinations were probably too strong," said Reggie.

"Now you're being personal, and possibly sarcastic," said the Babe with dignity. "I must go to bed. I was late last night."

"The night is yet young, Babe," said Stewart.

"So am I. But if I don't go, I shall continue to drink whisky and soda, and smoke."

"You are welcome. How is the tripos work progressing?"

"Oh, it's getting on," said the Babe, hopefully. "A little at a time, you know, but often. I'm not one of those people who can work five hours at a stretch."

"I suppose not. Is it to be a second or a third?"

"I believe there are three classes in the tripos," said the Babe stiffly. "You have only mentioned two. Well, yes, perhaps one of your small cigarettes would not hurt me. But I must go at eleven, because I am sapping. Oh, isn't that the *Shop Girl* on the table? There are some awfully good songs in it. May I go and get my banjo?"

"Do. I got it expressly for you to sing."

The Babe slept his usual eight and a half hours that night. He did not awake till 10.30.

XX
The Babe's Minor Diversions

> Where three times slipping from the outside edge
> I bumped the ice into three several stars.
> Tennyson.

The frost continued, black and clean, and the Babe, like the Polar Bear, thought it would be nice to practise skating. He bought himself a pair of Dowler blades with Mount Charles fittings, which he was assured by an enthusiastic friend were the only skates with which it was possible to preserve one's self-respect, and fondly hoped that self-respect was a synonym for balance. Hitherto his accomplishments in this particular line had been limited to what is popularly known as a little outside edge, but Reggie who was a first-rate skater undertook his education. The Babe, however, refused to leave his work altogether alone, for he was beginning to be seriously touched with the sapping epidemic, and he and Reggie used to set off about one, taking lunch with them, to the skating club, of which Reggie was a member, and of which the Babe was not.

Sykes only went with them once, and he would not have gone then, had it been possible to foresee that he would put skates in the same category as croquet balls and bathers, but it was soon clear that he did. He made a bee-line for the unemployed leg of Professor Robertson, who was conscious of having done the counter rocking turn for the first time in his life without the semblance of a scrape, and brought him down like a rabbit shot through the head. The Babe hurried across to the assistance of the disabled scientist, and dragged Sykes away. But Sykes had his principles, and as he dared not use threats to the Babe, he implored, almost commanded him not to put on his skates.

"Sykes, dear, you are a little unreasonable," said the Babe pacifically. "Reggie, what are we to do with Sykes? There was nearly one scientist the less in this naughty world."

The cab in which they had driven up, was still waiting, and at Reggie's suggestion Sykes was put inside and driven back to the stable where he slept.

The Babe wobbled industriously about, trying to skate large, and not deceive himself into thinking that a three was finished as soon as he had made the turn, and Reggie practised by himself round an orange, waiting for a four to be made up, until the Babe ate it.

About the third day the Babe was hopelessly down with the skating fever, which went badly with the sapping epidemic. He took his skates round to King's in the evening, after skating all day, for the sapping epidemic was rapidly fleeing from him like a beautiful dream at the awakening, and skated on the fountain; he slid about his carpet trying to get his pose right; he put his looking-glass on the floor and corrected the position of the unemployed foot; he traced grapevines with a fork on the tablecloth and loops with wineglasses; he dreamed that he covered a pond with alternate brackets and rocking turns, and woke up to find it was not true; he even watered the pavement outside his rooms in order to get a little piece of ice big enough for a turn, with the only result that the bed-maker, coming in next morning, fell heavily over it, barking her elbow, and breaking the greater part of the china she was carrying, which, as the Babe said, was happily not his. Unfortunately, however, the porter discovered it, as he brought round letters, and ruthlessly spread salt thickly over it, while the baffled Babe looked angrily on from the window.

Snow fell after this, and the Babe proposed tobogganing down Market Hill. He talked it over with Reggie, and they quarrelled as to which was the top of the hill and which the bottom, "for it would never do," said the scrupulous Babe, "to be seen tobogganing up hill," and on referring the matter to a third person, it was decided that the hill was perfectly level, so that they were both right and both wrong, whichever way you chose to look at the question.

The King's Comby (which is an abbreviation for Combination and means Junior Combination Room, but takes place in quite a different apartment) went off satisfactorily. The Babe, secure in the knowledge that there was no rhyme to Babe in the English language (his other name, which I have omitted to mention before, was Arbuthnot, and it would require an excess of ingenuity to find a rhyme even to that), made scurrilous allusions, most of them quite unfounded, about his friends, in vile decasyllables, and enjoyed himself very much. Later in the evening he with two of the performers in the original play acted a short skit on the *Agamemnon*, in which he parodied himself with the most ruthlessly realistic accuracy, and killed Agamemnon in a sponging tin with the aid of a landing net and a pair of scissors. Last of all he disgraced himself by stamping out in the snow, in enormous letters, the initials of a popular and widely known don of the college, with such thoroughness, that the grass has never grown since, and the initials are to be seen to this day, to witness if I lie. The proceedings terminated about three in the morning, and the Babe was left waiting for some minutes outside the porter's lodge at Trinity, while that indignant official got out of bed to open the gate to him.

The Babe ought to have caught a bad cold, but with an indefensible miscarriage of justice, it was the porter who caught cold, and not he, and the Babe observed cynically, when he heard of it, that the memory of the dog in the nursery rhyme, that bit a man from Islington in the leg, and then died itself, had at last been avenged.

Christmas, the Babe announced, fell early that year, and consequently he with several others stayed up till Christmas Eve, when they were allowed to stay no longer. He had gone up to town for two days to play in the University Rugby match, which he had been largely instrumental in winning, for the ground was like a buttered ballroom floor, a state of things which the Babe for some occult reason delighted in, and for an hour's space he proceeded to slip and slide and gloom and glance in a way that seemed to paralyse his opponents, and resulted in Cambridge winning by two tries and a dropped goal. The dropped goal was the Babe's doing: theoretically it had been impossible, for he appeared to drop it out of the middle of a scrimmage, but it counted just the same, and he had also secured one of the tries. The *Sportsman* for December 15th gives a full account of the match; also the Babe's portrait, in which he looks like a cross between a forger and a parricide.

On returning to Cambridge, in order to be up to date, he and some friends went out carol-singing one night, visiting the heads of colleges, and the houses of the married fellows. The Babe acted as showman and spoke broad Somersetshire, which interested a certain philologist, who had no suspicion that they were not town people, very much. The Babe declared that his father and grandfather had lived in Barnwell all their lives, and that he himself had never even attempted to set foot out of Cambridgeshire except once on the August Bank Holiday, when he had intended to go to Hunstanton but had missed the train. At this point, however, the philologist winked and said: "Mr. Arbuthnot, I believe." They collected in all seventeen shillings and eightpence, which they settled should be given to a local charity, but the Babe, as he counted the amount over with trembling, avaricious fingers, looked up with a brilliant smile as he announced the total and exclaimed: "Not a penny of that shall the poor ever see." They also got what Rudyard Kipling calls "lashings of beer" at several houses, and Bill Sykes who had been coached to carry a small tin into which offerings of money were put by the open-handed householder, was without a shadow of reason filled with so uncontrollable a fit of rage at the sight of the cook at one of the houses in Selwyn Gardens, who patted him on the head, and called him a pretty dear, that he dropped the tin mug, and nipped her shrewdly in the parts about the ankle.

Reggie parted from the Babe at the station, the latter going to London, and Reggie to Lincolnshire. The Babe travelled first because he said Sykes refused to go second or third, but that intelligent animal, poking his nose out from under the seat just as the guard was taking the tickets, was ignominiously hauled out, and compelled to go in the van, which cannot be considered as a class at all.

XXI
A DAY IN THE LENT TERM

O this drear March month.
Kingsley.

Jack Marsden stopped for a moment under the Babe's window and called

and the Babe's face looked out vindictively.

"If you call me like that I sha'n't answer," he said. "You're not in Clare."

So Jack went in, and found the Babe curled up again in a large chair, close to the fire, working. The month was February, which is equivalent, at Cambridge, to saying that it was raining—cold, sleety, impossible rain. As the exact day of the month was the sixteenth, it followed as a corollary that it had been raining for at least sixteen days, and, as it was leap year, it would continue to rain thirteen more.

"Well?" said the Babe unencouragingly. He had gone to bed early the night before, and the consequent length of the morning made him rather cross.

"Oh nothing. It's raining, you know. The *Sportsman* says that Jupiter Pluvius is in the ascendant still."

> "He sends the snow in summer,
> He sends the frost in May
> To nip the apple-blossoms,
> And spoil our games of play,"

quoted the Babe.

"Just so, and he doesn't neglect to send the rain in February. I've just come back from King's. Reggie's in a bad temper, almost as bad as you."

"Why?"

"Weather, chiefly. He says it would be grovelling flattery to call it beastly."

"Reggie is given to making truisms," said the Babe turning over the page. "Jack, I wish you'd go away. I want to work. Besides, you're so devilish cheerful, and I'm not."

"Sorry to hear it. Oh, yes, and Reggie told me to remind you that you are playing tennis with him at twelve. He's got the New Court."

The Babe brightened up: there was an hour less of morning.

"Hurrah! that will suit me excellently. Many thanks, and please go away. Good-bye."

Stewart confessed that the Babe had surprised him. Most people who knew the Babe were never surprised at him, because they always expected him to do something unexpected. But no one had ever supposed that he would do anything so unexpected as to work steadily every day. It would not have been so surprising if he had worked twelve hours a day twice a week, but that he should work four hours every day, upset all preconceived ideas about him. He had done so for a full month, and really there seemed no reason now why he should stop. He got up before nine, and he worked from ten till one: at one he would be himself again till six, but he would work from six till seven. Stewart considered this exhibition as a striking imitation by Nature of Mr. R. L. Stevenson's Jekyll and Hyde: he had not clearly realised before that the Babe had a dual nature. Just now he considered Hyde to be painfully predominant, for that the Babe should cease being absurd for four hours a day seemed to him a sacrifice of the best possibilities of his nature.

But the Babe, like Mr. Gladstone in one thing more, threw off all thoughts of such matters, except during work hours, and having determined to put in an extra hour in the afternoon, to make up for tennis in the morning, he trotted off through the dripping, drizzling rain to the tennis court in the best of spirits.

He went back to lunch with Reggie in King's Hall and as, contrary to all precedent, the rain had stopped, they went for a walk afterwards round two or three football grounds, to see what was going on, and give Mr. Sykes an airing. Scratch games seemed the order of the day, and they "took situations" on outside wings opposite each other for a few minutes in the game on the King's ground, until Reggie charged the Babe and knocked him down, after which they retired, dirty, but invigorated. Then they turned into the tennis court again for a while, and so by Burrell's Walk across the town bridge, and back into Trinity Street, looked in at the shop windows, which are perhaps less alluring than any others in the kingdom, and admired the preparations for diverting the sewerage of the town from the Cam.

"But how," said the Babe, "our college boats will be able to row in a perfectly empty river bed, is more than I feel fit to tell you."

"They'll keep up the water by shutting the locks," said Reggie, vaguely.

"But no shutting of locks, Reggie, will ever repair the drought caused by the cessation of the drains. There's the Master of Trinity. Take off your hat: he won't see you. I really wish Sykes wouldn't always smell Masters of colleges. It makes them nervous; they think indirectly that it's my fault. Bill, you idiot, come here!"

Bill having come to the conclusion that there were not sufficient grounds to warrant the Master's arrest, reluctantly dismissed the case, though he would have liked bail, and trotted after the Babe. The latter had just discovered that life was not worth living without a minimum thermometer which he saw in a chemist's window, and had to go and buy it.

They passed up to the left of Whewell's Court, by the churchyard without a church, and into Jesus Lane in order to deposit Sykes again at his stables, and then, as tea-time was approaching, turned back towards Trinity.

"And for our tea," said the Babe, "we will go to the Pitt, where it may be had cheaply and comfortably, and we can read the telegrams, which as far as I have observed, deal exclusively with steeplechase races, and the state of the money market. I noticed that money was easier yesterday. I am so glad. It has been terribly difficult lately. But if it is easier, no doubt the financial crisis between me and my father, which I expect at the end of this term, will be more capable of adjustment. At present I fear my creditors will find me like moist sugar, fourpence the pound. Do you suppose there are any races going on at Newmarket? We might drive over: I feel as if a little carriage exercise would do me good. Here's Jim. Jim always knows about races. He was born, I mean dropped, at Esher. Jim, is there any racing going on at Newmarket? Why do you look so disgusted?"

"It's so likely that flat races should be going on now," said Jim.

"Oh, well, it can't be helped," said the Babe. "What nice brown boots you've got. Have you been out on your gee-gee?"

"Looks rather like it."

"I thought so," said the Babe. "We're going to have tea. Do you know Reggie? Jim, Reggie, Reggie, Jim."

"Met before," said Jim. "Ta, ta, Babe. I've got a coach at four."

The Babe according to custom weighed and measured himself, found as usual that no change had taken place since yesterday, put his hat on the head of the bust of Pitt, whence it clattered on to the floor, let the door into the smoking room swing to in Reggie's face, and ordered tea. A group of three or four men before the fire were talking about someone called Pocohantas, who turned out on enquiry to be a horse, and the Babe expressed himself willing to lay current odds about anything in the world.

He and Reggie strolled back in the dusk, and parted at the gate of Trinity. The Babe went to work till Hall, and after Hall played picquet with Anstruther, whom he fleeced, capotting him once and repiquing him twice in an hour, and discussed with him the extraordinary dulness of the Lent term, and the impossibility of making it any livelier.

"It's a sort of close time," said the Babe, "for things of interest. I don't know why it should be so, but every day is exactly like every other day, and they are all dull. I feel eclipsed all the Lent term. I make a show of gaiety, but it is all hollow. I suppose really one does depend a good deal on things like cricket and football, and fine weather. One doesn't know it at the time, but one misses them when they are not there."

"You've taken to sapping: you oughtn't to mind."

"On the contrary I mind all the more. When I've done a morning's work, I come out fizzing with being corked up so long, and nothing happens to my fizz. It loses itself in the empty and infinite air."

"Don't be poetical, Babe."

"For instance," continued the Babe, "what am I to do now? I've had enough picquet, and I've got nothing to say, and I've worked enough, and I don't want to go to bed."

"All right, don't go to bed. Sit and talk to me."

"But I don't want to talk," said the Babe volubly. "There's nothing to talk about. I've played tennis, I've worked, I've taken Sykes for a walk, and that's all. Really one must be extraordinarily clever to be able to talk day after day all one's life. How does one do it? *A priori*, one would expect to have said all the things one has got to say by the time one was twenty, and I'm twenty-one. Yet I am not dumb yet. One doesn't talk about things that happen, and most people, and I am one myself, never think at all, so they can't talk about what they are thinking about. Give me some whisky and soda; perhaps, as Mulvaney says, it will put a thought into me. I hate Mulvaney worse than I hate Learoyd, and that is worse than I hate Ortheris. As for Mrs. Hawksbee, that's another story. Soda is like a solution of pin points. It pricks one all over the mouth. I wonder if it would do as well to put ordinary pins into water. I shall ask Longridge what he thinks about it. Now he's an exception, he does nothing but think; you can hear the machinery clicking inside him. He thinks about all the ingenious things he's going to do and all the ingenious things nobody else would think of doing. They don't come off mostly, because the door hits him in the face, or the gum won't stick. Thanks. When! Do you know Stewart is beginning to think I shall get through the tripos, and he warned me not to work too much. He says that I shall, by all precedents in such matters, get brain fever and consumption, and that my sorrowing friends will kneel round my expiring bedside—you see what I mean—on the morning the tripos lists are announced and shout out above the increasing clamour of my death rattle, 'You are Senior Historian,' and that my reform from the wild young spark to the pale emaciated student, will all date from one evening last year at the Savoy, when he said he would only take the longest odds if he had to bet on my getting through."

"And did you give him long odds?"

"No: I wouldn't have bet against myself even then, for the simple reason that one never knows how much one can try until one has tried. If you don't believe in yourself, nobody will believe in you. Not that I do believe in myself for a moment, any more than I believe in, in anybody else. You see, six months ago I shouldn't have believed it possible that I should work steadily four hours or more a day. I think I shall take to spectacles, and go for grinds on the Grantchester road; I believe that's the *chic* thing to do in sapping circles. Fancy waking up some morning to find oneself in a sapping circle. I wonder what Saps think about."

"Sap, probably. Oh, yes, certainly sap. Either Thucydides, or binomial theories, or is it theorems or aortas. Babe, let us meditate on aortas for a time."

"By all means. I wonder what an aorta is. Yes, thanks, but only a mouthful, as Reggie says. That's because he has such a big mouth. I say, I wish I had an object in life: it must be so interesting."

"Liver," said Anstruther brutally, "take a pill. What do you want an object in life for?"

"Oh, I don't know. It would be something to play about with, when one didn't want to talk or see other people. I suppose a conscience would do as well. I haven't either."

"You said ten minutes ago that you didn't want to talk. Since then I have only been able to get in an occasional word edgewise."

The Babe laughed, and finished his whisky.

"Yes, I'm very sorry. It's a great misfortune not to be able to be silent. It's not my fault. I sha'n't take a pill; I shall go to bed instead. I always used to think that 'the grave as little as my bed' was an independent sentence and meant literally what it said. Not that it meant much. Do you ever lie awake?"

"No, of course not: I can understand the difficulty of keeping awake, but not of going to sleep."

"I lay awake nearly five minutes last night," said the Babe, "and so I thought I was going to be ill! But I wasn't, at least not at present. I suppose people who lie awake, think."

"I always fancied they only swore."

"In that case there would be nothing gained. I'm getting silly. Good-night."

XXII
BEFORE THE TRIPOS

And when the bowler sent a ball
Off which none else would try to score,
He did not seem to care at all,
But hit it very high for four.
Hotch-potch Verses.

The Babe was lying at the bottom of a Canadian canoe on his back, singing low to his beloved. At least he was not exactly singing, but swearing gently at Sykes, who had laid himself down on his stomach and the day was too hot to have bulldogs on one's stomach. The Babe about an hour ago had landed to see if Reggie was in, and finding his rooms empty and ungarnished, tied his canoe up to the bank to sleep and read a little *Ravenshoe* for an hour, but it had slipped its cable and as he had left the paddle on the bank it had required only a few moments reflection to convince him that he was hopelessly and completely at the mercy of the winds and waters, like Danaë, the mother of Perseus, in her wooden chest, and that his destiny was no longer in his own hands. As then, there was nothing whatever to be done, he did nothing in serene content. He would soon bump against the arches of Clare Bridge, but until that happened there was no step he could possibly take.

It was just three days before his tripos began, and the Babe, with a wisdom beyond his years, was taking three complete holidays. He argued that as it already seemed to him that his brain was one turbid mass of undigested facts and dates, the best thing he could do was not to swallow more, but to let what he had settle down a little. For a fortnight before he had been working really hard, going over the ground again, and for the next three days he meant neither to think nor do anything whatever. As he expressed it himself after last Sunday morning chapel, "I am going," he said "to eat and sleep and do and be simply that which pleases me."

He was roused by a loud injured voice not far off shouting, "Look ahead, sir," and he sat up. His boat, as is the ineradicable habit of Canadian canoes, had drifted broadside across the river and was fouling the course of an outrigger which was wanting to come up.

"I'm very sorry," shouted the Babe, "but I've lost my paddle. Hallo, Feltham, is that you?"

"It's me, Babe. What can I do for you, and what do you mean by fouling my waterway? Where is your paddle?"

The Babe looked round.

"Oh, it's up there on the bank, by the King's Bridge. Can't I catch hold of the tail of your boat, then you might tow me up there?"

"All right, but don't call it a tail, as some rowing man will hear you and have a fit. Let me get clear. Are you slacking, to-day?"

"Yes, and for the next two days. My tripos begins on Monday, and I think that if I do nothing for a day or two I may be able to remember again who the Electric Sophia was."

"Is she important? She sounds as if she might be the wife of the man who discovered lightning."

"Don't confuse me further," said the Babe. "Where are you off to?"

"Oh, up the river. There's no cricket to-day."

"I didn't know that people who played cricket ever rowed."

"They don't for the most part: but I don't consider that a reason for not doing so if I wish."

"Are you playing for the 'Varsity on Monday?"

"They have been polite enough to ask me."

"And you have very civilly consented. Well, good-bye."

The Babe sat in his canoe for half an hour or more, and got through a little *Ravenshoe*, and a little meditation. The meditation concerned itself chiefly with Feltham, who, as was universally acknowledged, was the best of good fellows, quiet, steady, thoroughbred. And these things gave the Babe some pleasure not ill-deserved, to think over, for Feltham had been known primarily as a friend of his. And when he was tired of meditating he tied up his canoe again and walked up to the King's field, for his college was playing King's and he was certain of finding company, whichever side was in. It turned out that King's was in that enviable position, and of King's, Reggie and a careful little man in spectacles. Reggie could not by the most partial of his friends be called a cricketer, but the most impartial of his enemies would have had to confess that he often made a great many runs.

He had a good eye, he saw the ball and he helped it to fulfil its destiny by hitting it hard. More particularly did he hit balls on the off which ought to be left alone, and he always hit them high in the air over long slip's head. It really did not seem to matter where long slip was placed, for he always hit the ball over his head, and out of reach. Straight balls he subjected to a curious but very vigorous mowing process, which took them swiftly past the umpire's nose. A straight yorker invariably got him out, if he knew it was a yorker and tried to play it, so that when he saw one coming he held his bat perfectly firm and rigid and quenched it, but if it did not occur to him that the ball was a yorker he treated it with cheerful contempt and hit it somewhere, which surprised no one more than himself. It seemed to be the recognised thing that he should be given three lives as at pool, and, as at pool, if he used them up quickly, he was frequently allowed to star, and have two more. A sort of extra square leg, specially designed for his undoing, had just given him his fourth life when the Babe appeared, and Reggie scored three runs over it. The field luckily could be arranged solely with a view to catching him, for the careful little man in spectacles only scored singles, and those by hitting balls with extreme caution just out of reach of cover-point.

The Babe enjoyed watching cricket, especially the sort of game that was going on now. One bowler was extremely fast, the other incredibly slow, and Reggie hit them both in the air with perfect impartiality, and the careful little man played them both with as much precision and delicacy, as if he was playing spillikins.

However, a few overs later, though his own score was small, he did Reggie, and so, indirectly his side, a signal service. The latter had hit a fast ball almost quite straight up in the air and extremely high, and they both started on a forlorn run. Point and wicket-keep both ran to it, and the careful little man charged violently in between them exactly at the crucial moment, as they were both standing in front of his wickets, with the result that out of the midst of chaotic confusion the ball fell innocuously to the ground. The careful little man went to the pavilion for a new pair of spectacles after being given "not out" for obstructing the field, which he certainly had been doing, and point and wicket-keep cursed him and each other, and Reggie thanked them all.

This was the last ball of the over, so Reggie still had the bowling. The slow bowler prepared for him a ball with an immeasurable break from the off upon it, but Reggie very wisely danced gaily out onto the middle of the pitch, turned straight round and hit it so severe a blow that the wicket-keep in whose direction it was travelling had only just time to get out of the way.

It narrowly missed Reggie's own wicket, but a miss is as good as four runs when it is hit hard enough, and this one was.

But the service he often did his side, and was doing now, could not be fairly measured merely by the runs he scored, for the demoralising effect he always had on the field was worth fifty extra. After a certain number of catches have been missed, and a large number of balls hit high in the air just out of reach of a field, a side begins unconsciously to think "Kismet" and withal to grow discontented, and a side that thinks "Kismet" is lost.

Reggie was out seventh wicket down, having made sixty-two, and as there was only another half-hour to the drawing of stumps, he left the game, and walked down with the Babe. They were going to dine together and go to the theatre to see a touring *Mrs. Tanqueray*. To the Babe's great delight the "theatrical tuft-hair" was in great force, and between the acts he wandered about in the passage listening rapturously to the fragments of their conversation.

There was one in particular, who had sat next the Babe, markedly worthy of study. His gown was about eighteen inches long, and his cap, out of which he had carefully abstracted every particle of board, drooped gracefully at all its corners. He was in dress clothes with a smoking coat (not in a Norfolk jacket,) and he wore a large diamond solitaire, and a red cummerbund. He was evidently a king among his kind, and several of them crowded round him as he came out between the acts and admired him. They called him "Johnny," and he called them "Johnny" individually, and "Johnnies" collectively, and the Babe listened to them with a seraphic expression of face.

"Arfly parful, isn't it? I say, Johnny, give me a light."

"Old Redfarn's put up a notice about not smoking in the passage. I shall rag him about it."

"That gurl's pretty good, isn't she? Looks rather nice too."

"You're quite mashed on her, old chappie. But she's not a patch on Mrs. Pat."

"Johnny can't think of anything but Mrs. Pat. I say, let's go and have a drink."

"All right. Johnny stands drinks. The gurl at the bar's an awful clipper."

"Johnny will drop his pipe and get her to pick it up for him."

"Well, come on, you Johnnies. There's only ten minutes. Keep an eye on Johnny."

The Babe's eye followed them as they walked off to the bar, with rapturous enjoyment.

"Aren't they heavenly?" said he to Reggie. "Oh, I wish I was like that! It must be so nice to feel that one is the light and leading of the whole place and really knows what life is. I wish I knew what life was. I wonder how they get their hair to stick out like that. How I have wasted my time! I too might have been a Johnny by now, if I'd cultivated them. Reggie, do come to the bar: I want to gaze and gaze on them."

But Reggie refused: he said they made him sick, and the Babe told him that he regarded things from the wrong standpoint.

"You know," said the Babe, "they've persuaded each other that they are the very devils of fellows. They really believe it. What a thing it is to have faith. They will talk quite fluently to the barmaid. I remember so well trying to see whether I could. I couldn't: I knew I couldn't all the time. I have never felt so hopelessly bored in so few minutes. They think it's wicked; and they think that they rag their tutors. The poor tutors are men of no perception, for they haven't the least idea they are being ragged. There they all come again. Their faces shine with deviltry. Did you hear them talk about Mrs. Pat? They meant Mrs. Patrick Campbell you know—"

"You're no better, Babe," said Reggie, "you used to want people to think you wicked."

"Oh, but that's quite different. You can't say that I was ever the least like a Johnny. I never had the courage. Fancy being as brave as they are, and oh, fancy deliberately sitting down and taking all the stuffing out of your cap in order to be a blood!"

"I'll take yours out, if you'll take mine, Babe. There's the bell. We must go in again."

The Babe went to see Stewart when he went back to Trinity. The latter thoroughly approved of his holiday.

"You are giving yourself a little space," he said, "in which it may be hoped you will forget, or rather assimilate, a few of the useless and ugly things which our system of examinations has compelled you to learn. A historian is not a person who knows masses of facts and dates, but a man who has built a structure upon them. The facts are the scaffold, which disappears when the house is built. And the tripos turns out a quantity of promising young men who can only build scaffolds. I wish I was examining.

There should be no questions with dates in them, and they should all begin "Trace the tendency," or "Indicate in a great many words the influence."

"I wish I felt more certain about my scaffold."

"My dear Babe, don't vex your soul. Possess it in peace. I would give long odds on your getting through. What I did not expect was that you should have taken the distasteful steps that lead to so immaterial a result. You got a second in your last May's didn't you? Do let us talk of something a little more interesting than triposes."

"Well, I didn't introduce the subject," said the Babe.

"What have you been doing this evening?"

"I've just been to the *Second Mrs. Tanqueray* with Reggie."

"An interesting medical case," remarked Stewart. "I believe the author consulted an eminent nerve doctor, as to how many months' living with Aubrey Tanqueray would drive an excitable female to suicide. He thought six, but as the author wished her to do it in less, he had to introduce other incentives. Aubrey Tanqueray would drive me to madness in a week, and to suicide in eight days. He handed her toast at the scene at breakfast, as if he was giving her a slice of some cardinal virtue with the blessing of the Pope spread on it like butter. The real *motif* of the play, though the British public haven't known it, is her growing despair at being wedded to him, and the immediate cause is the *Second Mr. Tanqueray's* noble forgiveness of her when she was found to have tampered with the letter bag. He treated her like a candidate for confirmation, instead of boxing her ears, and said that the incident only served to draw them closer together, or something of the kind. Apparently if you commit a sufficiently mean action towards a person who really loves you, he will be delighted, and love you the more for it. It sounds a little Jesuitical, baldly stated. Who wrote the play? Pinero wasn't it. Pinero is obviously the future from 'Pinsum,' I am a pin."

The Babe laughed.

"I didn't attend to the play much," he said. "There was an undergraduate sitting next me, who was more interesting. He wore a red cummerbund."

"Ah, yes," murmured Mr. Stewart. "The kind that talks to the female in tobacconists' shops, and sits on the counter as it does so. Its father is usually one of nature's gentlemen, who has married a perfect lady. The two always marry each other, and in the next generation the females dress in Liberty fabric, and the males congregate at the smaller colleges. They are on the increase. I suppose it's an instance of the survival of the filthiest."

Mr. Stewart rose from his chair, and crossed over to the window-seat where the Babe was sitting.

"What can I do to amuse you, Babe?" he said. "I feel that it is the duty of all your friends to distract your thoughts from all subjects for the next two days. Shall I play cards with you—you shall teach me—or shall we talk about the Epsom meeting, or the A.D.C.? I suppose you are going to act in the May week? Why not act *Hamlet*, and we will persuade Longridge to be Ophelia. There is something sublimely inconsequent in the way Ophelia distributes artificial flowers to the company which reminds me of Longridge in his soberer moments. I have been very much tried by Longridge to-night. He asked me to help him to sing glees in the Roundabout. Can you imagine Longridge and me sitting side by side in the Roundabout singing "Three Blind Mice?" I could imagine it so vividly that I didn't go."

The Babe laughed.

"You can give me whisky and soda, and then I shall go to bed. It is twelve, and I must practise being dressed and breakfasted by nine. Does it require much practice?"

"I should think about twenty minutes every morning. What is the use of doing a thing you have got to do, before you have got to do it? It is like cutting yourself with a knife to accustom yourself to a surgical operation."

"There are points of similarity," said the Babe. "I shall go to bed now for all that, as soon as I've drunk this."

XXIII
The Lists

List, O list.
Shakespeare.

The Babe and Reggie were sitting outside the pavilion at Fenner's watching the University against the gentlemen of England, who as the Babe said, so far from sitting at home at ease were running out to Feltham's slow bowling and getting caught and stumped, with very enjoyable frequency. The cricket was a delightful mixture of a fine bowling performance and very hard hitting, which to the uneducated spectator is perhaps the most lively of all to watch. Feltham had in fact, from the Babe's point of view, just sent down the ideal over. The first ball was hit out of the ground for six, the second bowled the hitter round his legs. The third ball was hit by the incomer for four, and the fourth for four. The fifth ball he also attempted to hit as hard as he could to square leg, and he was caught at point, in the manner of a catch at the wicket.

The Babe tilted his hat over his eyes, and gave a happy little sigh.

"Reggie, the tripos is the secret of life," he said. "If you want to get a real feeling of leisure and independence, a feeling that you have been told privately by the archangels to amuse yourself and do nothing whatever else, go in for the tripos, or rather wait till you come out. I suppose that considering my years I have wasted more time than most people, and I thought I knew what it felt like. But I didn't. I had no idea how godlike it is to do nothing. To have breakfast, and feel that it won't be lunch-time for four hours, and after that to have the whole afternoon before you."

"When are the lists out?"

"Oh, in about ten days now. Don't talk about lists. Tell me how long you worked this morning. Tell me about the man in your college who works ten hours every day and eleven hours every night. Tell me of the difficulty of learning by heart the Roman emperors or the kings of Israel and Judah. Assure me that by knowing the angle of the sun above the horizon and the length of Feltham's shadow, you could find out how tall the umpire is."

"He's about five foot ten," said Reggie.

"That's like the answers I used to give to the questions about the hands of a watch," said the Babe. "They tell you that if the hands of a watch are together at twelve—there's no 'if' about it, it is never otherwise,—when will they be together next. I always said about five minutes past one. It seems absurdly simple. I've often noticed them together-then: and the same remark applies to about ten minutes past two. That reminds me," added the Babe, looking at his watch, "that it's twenty-five minutes past five. The hour hand seems to have gained a little."

"Oh, I remember," said Reggie. "The hour hand gains seven-elevenths."

"Seven-elevenths of what?"

"I don't know. Of the answer, I suppose. I shouldn't have thought it was five yet."

"But it is, and that compels us to decide between tea and cricket."

"We can get tea in the pavilion. There's another four."

"You shall give me a hundred to one that the next ball is not a wicket," said the Babe.

"In pennies, and make it fifty."

"Done."

A very audible click, and an appeal. Reggie got up and felt in his pockets.

"I should have been ashamed to get out to a ball like that. You'll have to pay for tea, Babe. There you are."

"Twopence more," said the Babe.

"Not if I went to the stake for it, Hullo, Ealing, where are you from? Ealing's got a glorious post-tripos face too. He really deserves to be able to play 'Praise the Lord, ye heavens, adore Him,' but he can't even now."

"Composed by Mr. Haydn," said Ealing, "and performed by Mr. Ealing. It contains a very difficult passage. Your left hand has to go to the left, and your right hand to the right. You feel all pulled in two. Babe, the tripos is the noblest of inventions. I think I shall go in for a second part. I can quite understand how the lower classes get in such boisterous spirits on bank holidays that they change hats with each other."

"I'd change hats with—with a bishop," said the Babe, looking wildly about for suggestions.

"So would I. Or with Longridge. He wears a blue cake hat. Hullo, they're all out."

"Come and have tea, then," said Reggie. "The Babe stands tea."

"Hang the expense," said the Babe, recklessly. "When a man's got some tin, what can he do better than to give his pals a real blow out? I've got four shillings. Tea for three, and bread and butter for two. The fortune of the Rothschilds sprang from these small economies. Bread and butter for two will be plenty. I'm sure none of us can be very hungry on so warm a day. Oh, there's a tuft-hair drinking out of a tall glass. I expect it's gin-sling. What is gin-sling? In any case you can't say it ten times. Ging-slin."

"I thought you could always say Ranjitsinghi, Babe."

"I can when other people are just unable to. Sufficient champagne gives me a wonderful lucidity, followed by sleepiness. There's Stewart. I didn't know he came to cricket matches."

Stewart was delighted to see them.

"But you, Babe, are not fit for the society of ordinary people," he said, "your extreme cheerfulness since your tripos argues a want of consideration for others. What have you been doing?"

"I've been looking at cricket, and also talking."

"You don't say so."

"I have, indeed," said the Babe. "What effect does champagne have on you?"

"Why do you ask these sudden questions?" said Stewart wearily. "It makes the wings of my soul sprout."

"The principle is the same. I ate lobster salad the other day and drank port. It did not give me indigestion, but acute remorse."

"Remorse for having done so?"

"No, a vague searching remorse for all the foolish things I had done, and all the foolish things I meant to do, and for being what I was. Food doesn't affect your body, it affects your soul. Conversely, sermons which are supposed to affect your soul make you hungry."

Stewart lit a match thoughtfully against the sleeve of his coat.

"The Babe has hit on a great truth," he said. "A curious instance occurred to my knowledge two years ago. A strong healthy man read *Robert Elsmere*. It gave him so severe an attack of dyspepsia that he had to spend the ensuing winter on the Riviera and eat pepsine instead of salt for eighteen months. Then he died. The phenomenon is well established. Poor Simpson, the fellow of my college, as you know, broke his leg the other day. It was supposed to have happened because he tripped and fell downstairs. But he told me himself that he was just leaving his room, and that as he walked down stairs he read the first few pages of *Stephen Remarx*. It was that, of course, that broke his leg, and so he fell down stairs as soon as he tried to put it to the ground. The Babe is quite right. Sermons, as he told us, make him hungry and lobster and port remorseful. In the same way, high tea, if frequently taken, will make anyone a non-conformist, in the same way as incense induces Roman Catholicism. But, Babe, don't tell Longridge."

"Why not?"

"He will want to talk about it to me, and then I shall be taken with melancholy madness. Are you coming up for another year, Babe?"

"I don't know. I should like to. Of course it will depend on my getting through. If I do, I think a note from my tutor to my father might have a wholesome effect."

"Your tutor will do whatever you wish him to," said Stewart. "At present he is going back to college. I have a hansom waiting because I hate walking. Do any of you want a lift?"

The others stayed up till stumps were drawn, and walked down together. The tea no doubt had affected the Babe's soul in some subtle manner, producing acute fatuity.

The Babe spent the remaining ten days in assiduous inaction. He sat in canoes, he sat on benches watching cricket, he ate, he slept. He appeared at the Senate house on the morning when the lists were read out, in pumps, in pink pyjamas, a long great-coat, and a straw hat. Reggie, who stood next him, thought he detected signs of nervousness, when the names began to be read, but it is probable that he was mistaken, for the Babe had never before been known to be afflicted with that distressing malady. A large number of his more intimate friends were there, and an air of suspense was abroad. But it was over sooner than any one anticipated, for the Babe, contrary to the expectation of even the most sanguine of them all, and that was himself, came out first in the second class. There was one moment's pause of astonishment, not unmingled with awe, and then a wild disorderly scene of riot and shouting arose, in which the Babe was seized and taken back to Trinity in a triumphal procession, which carried him over the grass in the great court, wholly disregarding the porters who gibbered helplessly around them, until Stewart appeared, who, however, instead of instantly stopping it, seemed to take sympathetic interest in the proceeding.

Later in the day he wrote a charming letter to the Babe's father, in which he congratulated him on his son's brilliant success, alluded to his keen historical instinct and his vivid grasp of events—whatever a vivid grasp may be—and stated (which was undoubtedly true), that if certain five men out of the whole University had not happened to go in for the same tripos the same year, the Babe would infallibly have been Senior Historian.

An answer came later to Stewart and the Babe. The latter's was short but satisfactory. Reggie was breakfasting with him when the post came in, or rather he was waiting without any excess of patience while the Babe, whom he had just pulled out of bed, explained precisely how it was that he was not dressed yet, and urged him not to begin, or if he insisted on doing so, to play fair.

At this moment the porter entered with the letter, and the Babe snatched it from his hand, tore it open, and executed a *pas seul* round the room, until he stepped on the kettle lid, and hurt himself very much.

"The Babe B.A. will be in residence another year," he shouted. "You may eat all the breakfast, if you like."

Reggie had a healthy appetite, and the Babe was rather plaintive about it.

Stewart, who had received a letter from the Babe's father by the same post, looked in after breakfast with congratulations.

"I am delighted," he said, "but, in a way, disappointed, and for this reason: I was looking forward to your *denoûement* with some interest, and I should have found a melancholy pleasure in seeing how you would make your exit from Cambridge, and what piece of extraordinary folly would have been your last. It seems I shall have to wait another year for that."

"Oh, don't mind me," said the Babe, shrilly. "Say you're sorry I'm coming up again straight out, if you like."

"No. On the whole, I don't mind waiting another year," said Stewart.

www.ingramcontent.com/pod-product-compliance
Lightning Source LLC
LaVergne TN
LVHW042155190726
843493LV00006B/1678